Wild Flowers *of the* Peak District

Text by
Patrick Harding

Art Editor
Valerie Oxley

The **Hallamshire** Press
2000

© 2000 The Hallamshire Press

Published by The Hallamshire Press Limited
Broom Hall
Sheffield S10 2DR
England

Typeset by The Hallamshire Press Limited
Printed in Singapore

All rights reserved. No part of this publication may be reproduced, stored in a retrieval system, or transmitted, in any form or by any means, electronic, mechanical, photocopying, recording or otherwise, without the prior permission in writing of the publishers.

British Library Cataloguing in Publication Data:
 A catalogue record for this book is available from the British Library.

ISBN 1 874718 53 9

Contents

Illustrators	4
Foreword	5
Preface	6
Botanical Illustration at the University of Sheffield	7
The Peak District	8
Wild Flowers of the Peak District	**17**
Glossary	138
Bibliography	139
Index of English Names	141
Index of Latin Names	143
General Index	144

Illustrators

Mary Acton
Jean Binney
Lionel Booker
Dorothy Bramley
Nancy Brockington
Ivy Brown
Geoffrey Copley
Jacqueline Dawson
Anne Dent
Sylvia Ford
Jennie Hinton
Jill Holcombe
Sue James
Shelley Jones
Primrose Lawton
Irene Mackerness
Valerie Oxley

Judy Pickles
Penni Ravenhill
Juliet Regan
Jan Relton
Trudy Roe
Pauline Snaith
Sheila Stancil
Cyril Stocks
Chrissie Vale
Margaret Wightman
Cate Wildman
Amanda Willoughby
Catherine Zurbrugg

Photographs by Patrick Harding except Cloudberry (Steve McCutcheon, FLPA—Images of Nature).

Foreword

My congratulations to all the artists who have obtained their Certificate in Botanical Illustration from the University of Sheffield. Judging by the beautiful illustrations in this book they have obviously been well taught in both art and botany. In an age of photography and electronic media not everyone realises how important the art of botanical illustration remains. One can show so much more of the characteristics of a plant through art and we botanists continue to use it as the preferred way to illustrate our descriptive works about plants.

The Peak District is one of my favourite places for walking and one of the joys is always the show of wild flowers throughout the year. I know that this book will encourage people to look at this interesting flora. Each illustration is accompanied by a most readable text that presents a host of interesting botanical information and fascinating general facts about each plant. Here is a book that will help to enhance many visits to the Peak District.

Professor Sir Ghillean Prance FRS, VMH
Director, Royal Botanic Gardens, Kew.

Preface

Wild Flowers of the Peak District is a celebration of the skill of some thirty botanical illustrators who have attended classes run by the University of Sheffield's Division of Adult Continuing Education, tutored by Valerie Oxley. It is however, not simply a collection of beautiful colour plates as the accompanying text helps to complete a fuller picture of each chosen species. Just as an animal photographer needs to know about the behaviour of a species to facilitate the taking of good photographs, so botanical illustrators require not only artistic skills but also knowledge of the plants being illustrated. Dr Patrick Harding (who supplied both the text and the photographs for this book) has taught elements of plant taxonomy, anatomy and biology to the artists as part of the Certificate in Botanical Illustration run by the University of Sheffield.

This book covers some 60 species in detail. The choice of species was based on a number of criteria. Firstly an attempt was made to select species from the range of different habitats found in the Peak District. Secondly plants were chosen from among the more common species which are likely to be seen by visitors to the area, and also selected from some of the rarer species. The plants are illustrated life size and this precluded many smaller species, the illustrations of which would have been too small for the large format chosen. Mindful of the law that bans the uprooting of any wild plant without the landowner's permission (and for some species even with permission) only the above ground parts have been depicted for most species. Some of the orchids have had their underground storage tubers painted—this information was not taken from uprooted plants but from herbarium and other source material.

The order of the 60 species follows the flowering year. The first few species can be found in flower as early as February and March, these are followed by the spring flowers and then those that are at their best in May and June. Many of the White Peak species flower early, before drought becomes a problem. In contrast the full colour of Heather on the Dark Peak is not apparent until August. Some species have a short flowering season but others may produce flowers over a period of several months and their order in the book is more arbitrary. Many species in the Peak District flower several weeks later than they do further south and plants such as Lesser Celandine, which will have finished flowering in many parts of southern England by May, can still be found flowering into July in the more upland parts of the Peak District.

The text for each species follows a similar layout. Both Latin and Common names are recorded together with the plant family to which the species belongs. Rules about family names now require them to be based on a constituent genus which is fine for the family Rosaceae, which includes the genus Rosa, but has led to the Cruciferae being renamed Brassicaceae (after the genus Brassica). Both the new and the more familiar family names have been included. Where there has been a recent change in the Latin name of a species both new and old names are recorded. Common names of some species are almost universal across Britain but others are much more local and where possible north midland local names have been included. Where names (Latin and English) carry information on aspects such as habitat, flower colour, medicinal and culinary use or folklore associations these have been mentioned.

Other sections deal with the preferred habitat of the species and the general distribution of the plant in the Peak District. Features that help to accurately identify the plant, including those such as scent and flowering season, which cannot be shown in the illustration, are included, as are the distinguishing features of similar species. Details of any common garden cultivars (cultivated varieties) are provided as some people will know these better than the wild types.

Botanical Illustration at the University of Sheffield

One warm Spring day in 1988 a phone call to Dr Patrick Harding, at the University of Sheffield's Division of Adult Continuing Education, set the seed for the blossoming of a unique partnership and programme of courses that neither the maker of the call, Valerie Oxley, or the recipient could have perceived or envisaged.

Dr Harding was interested in the concept of offering Botanical Illustration as a subject within his Natural History Programme at the University, but slightly cautious and concerned that recruitment and interest in the subject might not be forthcoming or sustained. Tentatively, a course in the basic techniques of Botanical Illustration was advertised in the Division's programme. Thirty six applications for the course were received and from that moment the seed began to grow!

The participants came from varying backgrounds. Alongside the specialists, who had previously studied art or science, there were keen gardeners, amateur naturalists and people who simply enjoyed looking at plants and flowers, wild or cultivated. There were people who, for one reason or another, had missed the chance to study at school and arrived with no formal qualifications or basic artistic skills. A diverse group brought together by a shared interest in plants, they were ready to learn, observe and record. Their enthusiasm for the subject was overwhelming.

Expectation was high and the atmosphere slightly charged at the first class, but the magic had begun. The participants began a voyage of discovery similar to the early expeditions by the intrepid plant hunters.

Interest grew and courses in Botanical Illustration were offered at various locations. There were dayschools in Barnsley, Bakewell and Doncaster, whilst longer courses were offered in Rotherham, Chesterfield, Worksop and Retford.

Meanwhile, Dr Harding was developing his own programme of courses concerned with the identification and understanding of plants. Students on the Botanical Illustration courses were curious to know more about the scientific structure and function of the plants, where they came from and how they grew. It seemed a natural move to link the two areas together and offer a course directly marrying the art with the science of the subject.

The Certificate in Botanical Illustration was launched in 1994, the course involved two years part-time study, equivalent to the first level of a degree. The practical artwork was taught by Valerie Oxley and the scientific programme by Patrick Harding. A week-end at Losehill Hall, the Peak District National Park Centre near Castleton, was included in the programme so that students had the opportunity to find and identify plants in the field.

The course was so successful that it was offered each year for the following four years and applications always exceeded the number of available places. A supporting accredited programme was established to prepare participants for the discipline of the more focused Certificate course. The programme was structured so that students could progress through the classes gaining confidence, botanical knowledge and artistic skills.

The progressive accredited route did not appeal to some of the early pioneers who attended the first classes. A few people preferred to continue painting for pleasure without the pressures of meeting deadlines and writing essays. Self-help groups were established around the City and beyond, made up of pockets of artists meeting together to share and enjoy their common interest in drawing and painting flowers. To our delight plant studies from some of these artists are included in this book.

In September 1998, the first Diploma course in Botanical Illustration was offered at the University of Sheffield. The illustration programme has evolved naturally, complementing the botany. Drawing is essential to understanding; it is the seeing eye, the tool of discovery.

Increased awareness of modern technology and access to the Internet has highlighted an amazing number of anomalies in the descriptions of plants. Students find themselves delving even deeper into the flowers, to examine the detail of their structures. Plants are researched, questions asked, opinions sought; there is scientific discussion, investigation and argument. Scientists from our major botanical institutions have been involved in some of the debate about the structure, form and function of the plants the students are illustrating. The quest for information and solutions is never-ending.

The interest in Botanical Illustration continues to flourish, it is a living art in the service of science.

The artists who have work illustrated within these pages are a small proportion of the many students who have attended the classes since 1988. The seed has grown into a tree of knowledge which continues to bear fruit. Students have exhibited their work at the Royal Horticultural Society, London and The Hunt Institute for Botanical Documentation, Pittsburgh, USA. There seems to be no limit to their enthusiasm and achievements. The common driving force is the desire to share the fun and friendship which comes from *simply painting flowers*!

Valerie Oxley

The Peak District

The Peak District lies at the southern end of the Pennines and is the meeting point for Highland Britain, to the north and west, and Lowland Britain, to the south and east. It is close to the centre of England and even its borders are at least 80 kms (c. 50 miles) from the sea. Much of the land is at an altitude of over 300 metres (c. 1,000 feet) and a few places exceed 600 metres (c. 2,000 feet).

To the east and west of this high ground is low-lying land—the Yorkshire and Nottinghamshire coal vales to the east and the Cheshire plain to the west. The Pennine southern flanks slope off gradually but in contrast the high ground to the north continues for many miles, making an easy demarcation of the Peak District impossible.

In 1951, a large part of the region was included in the Peak District National Park. The area delimited by this, Britain's first National Park is some 1,438 square kilometres (c. 555 sq. miles). The majority of the Peak National Park (as it is often called) lies in the county of Derbyshire but Staffordshire, Cheshire and Greater Manchester lay claim to parts of the western section, with South and West Yorkshire claiming some of the more northerly areas. While the term 'Peak District' was originally used for the upland area of Derbyshire, the National Park is not exclusive to Derbyshire even though many media reporters would have us think otherwise!

The term Peak District is itself something of a misnomer as much of the high ground, (which in places exceeds 600 metres) consists of a series of plateaux rather than distinctive peaks. The term originates from the Old English word 'peac' which means a knoll. Further confusion is added by the local terms High Peak and Low Peak. These areas are not easily defined and parts of Low Peak are at a higher altitude than some regions within High Peak! In general, High Peak (which is still retained as the name for the parliamentary ward) includes the high ground in the north of the Peak Park including much of the moorland but also the limestone areas north of Lathkill Dale. Low Peak includes the more southerly part of the limestone region and some of the surrounding areas.

No large towns are included within the National Park but Buxton, Leek and Matlock are all close to its boundaries as indeed is the city of Sheffield. Stoke, Manchester, Huddersfield, Nottingham and Derby are within easy travelling distance, with an estimated 17 million people living within 60 miles (c. 96 kms) of the Park boundaries. It has been calculated that there are up to 30 million visits made to the Peak Park every year, the majority between May and September, which corresponds to the flowering season for most of the plants mentioned in this book.

Map showing the position of the Peak District.

Factors Affecting the Distribution of Plants in the Peak District

Geographical Position

A number of plant species reach the edge of their distribution range in England. Certain southern European species are only found in the southern half of England and some of Britain's most northerly populations of plants such as Nettle-leaved Bellflower (*Campanula trachelium*) and Stemless Thistle (*Cirsium acaulon*) occur in the Peak District. Other species have a more northerly distribution, for example Cowberry (*Vaccinium vitis-idaea*) and Globe Flower (*Trollius europaeus*) both of which are close to their south-eastern limit in the Peak District.

Globe Flower (and a number of other species which are more frequent in the colder and wetter northern parts of Britain) is most frequent in shady, north and west-facing habitats in the Peak and is virtually absent from open, south-facing slopes. In contrast, Stemless Thistle is currently largely restricted to warm, open, south-facing sites. Research is still in progress to monitor populations of such plants that are near their geographical limits in the Peak. Climatic change, especially if it involves an increase in average temperatures and a change in rainfall pattern, could result in the Globe Flower retreating northwards such that it becomes extinct in the Peak. Equally, southern species such as Stemless Thistle might become more common and spread to sites that are not all south facing.

Climate

The geographical position of the Peak minimises the maritime climatic conditions that are found nearer the coasts of Britain and the area has something of a continental climate. In particular the high ground induces rain (or snow) fall from Atlantic depressions blown in from the Irish Sea.

The greatest annual rainfall, of over 150 cm (c. 59 inches) is recorded from the highest land, e.g. Kinder Scout near the north-western boundary, and this decreases (roughly in relation to declining altitude) to less than 90 cm (c. 35 inches) near the south-eastern border. Even this latter amount is higher than that occurring in most low-lying areas to the south and east of the Peak. As with many aspects of climate there are marked differences in rainfall amounts from sites only a few kilometres apart.

On the whole the Peak District receives less sunshine than the average for England. This is partly due to its position and elevation, with low cloud producing hill fog, but is also due to mists associated with temperature inversions in some of the valleys.

Temperature is also affected by altitude and generally temperature declines with increasing altitude. Only a few plant species grow actively at temperatures below 5.6°C (42°F) and in the colder, higher parts of the Peak there is a relatively short growing season. This is apparent to any gardener visiting the area and also means that the flowering season for many wild flower species in the Peak can be several weeks later than that in more southern, and western, parts of Britain. Temperature inversions, when cold air sinks to valley bottoms, are not uncommon in the High Peak and these can lead to harder frosts at lower altitudes—a reverse of the general trend. Temperature (and with it soil thaw after frost and snow lie) is also influenced by topography. In deep valleys and on north-facing sites not reached by the warmth of the sun, the effects of snow and frost will be longer lasting and the growing season will be shorter. In summer the soil of such areas will remain cooler and moister than that on south-facing slopes.

Geology

There are marked differences in the geology of different parts of the Peak District and these differences have had a huge influence on vegetation type and on the local distribution of many plant species. Most of the rocks at or near the surface of the Peak Park were formed during the Carboniferous era (some 350 million years ago) and are either limestones, shales or gritstones. (See map overleaf.)

The central and southern limestone mass forms a series of plateaux which rise from about 120 m (390 ft) in the south-east, to c. 300 m (1,000 ft) in the central region and up to 475 m (1,550 ft) at the northern and western end of the outcrop. Partly due to the colour of the limestone (though it is in fact more a creamy-grey) this region is known as the White Peak. Although limestone will slowly dissolve in rain-water, it is largely impervious to it, though water does percolate along the bedding planes and down the joints in the rock. As a result the rock stays dry and is not prone to frost shattering (where water expands on freezing and causes the rock to fragment) resulting in a gently undulating landscape.

Uplifting of the limestone country, to produce what is called the Derbyshire Dome, caused cracks and fissures in the limestone some of which were later filled with mineral ores including galena (lead sulphide) and fluorite (calcium fluoride). The vertical ore-filled fissures, many of which run in an east-west direction, are known as 'rakes' while deposits in the enlarged bedding planes (between the limestone deposits) are called 'flats' or 'pipes'.

The limestone plateaux are dissected by valleys known as dales. The term comes from the Norse word 'dair' meaning a valley. Some of these are quite shallow and dry, resulting from early erosion processes, or more recent weathering away of softer overlying shales. The more spectacular deeper dales were probably formed as a result of an uplifting of the land in the Pleiocene era (less than 10 million years ago) with streams and rivers subsequently cutting out the valleys. Water moving below the surface has widened the joints and bedding planes of the limestone into caverns and the eventual collapse of cavern roofs may have formed some of the more gorge-like dales.

The deeply incised dales reduced the level of the water table below that of the shallower dales thus resulting in most of the latter being 'dry' dales. This lowering of the water table was accentuated by the activities of 18th- and 19th-century lead miners who constructed 'soughs' (drainage channels) to reduce flooding in their mines. Limestone pavement, an element of limestone scenery which is such an important part of the Yorkshire Dales National Park (to the north of the Peak Park) is virtually absent from the Peak as the area was not scoured by the glacial action of the last Ice Age.

Most of the rest of the Peak Park is made up of bands of grey-black sedimentary shales and gritstones and these form the Dark Peak, an area shaped like an inverted horseshoe surrounding three sides of the White Peak. The shales are revealed in the Edale and Hope Valleys and on the lower slopes of the Millstone grit hills. Water is held between the rock particles in shale and when this freezes it causes rapid weathering thus resulting in a softly rounded landscape. The overlying gritstones (coarse sandstones) do not hold water and weather more slowly except in those places where the rapid weathering of the shales beneath has undermined the gritstones or where water in the joints and bedding planes has expanded on freezing and caused large blocks to break off. These processes have resulted in a series of inwardly facing, grey-black escarpments (known locally as 'edges') below which are areas of block scree, overlooking the limestone region.

Streams in the dark Peak have also cut valleys and these are known locally as 'cloughs'. Unlike many of the White Peak dales these are not cut below the water table and retain a permanent water course.

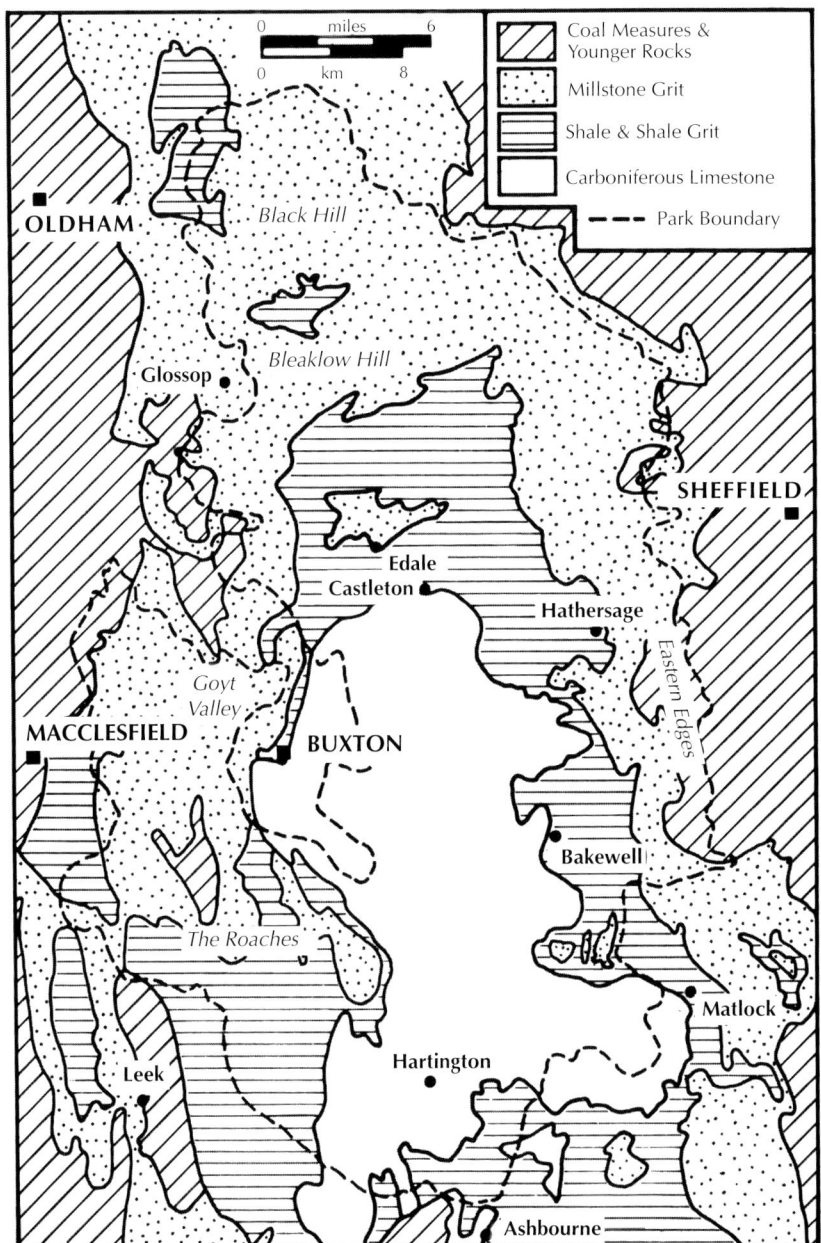

Map showing the surface geology of the Peak District.

Soils

With the exception of species growing on rock outcrops or stone walls, the local distribution of plants in the Peak District is more dependent on soil type rather than on the underlying geology. Nowhere is this more evident than on some higher parts of the limestone plateaux in the White Peak where a moderate rainfall has leached (washed) out the calcium, resulting in an acid soil capable of supporting lime-avoiding (calcifuge) species such as Heather (*Calluna vulgaris*) and Bilberry (*Vaccinium myrtillus*). Such limestone heathland was extensive, and even provided peat as a fuel source, until the early part of the 19th century, by which time most had been enclosed under the Enclosure Acts. Agricultural improvement, including liming, transformed the heathland to hay-meadows and pasture.

The bulk of the limestone plateau vegetation is now improved grassland (much of it re-seeded) and includes pasture land and meadows which are now mostly cut for silage. Unlike the hay-meadows of old there is little diversity of flowering plant species to be found here and most of the interesting and rare species are restricted to the sloping dale sides. Even in the dales the soils are far from uniform. This is in part due to windblown and other acidic material deposited on top of the limestone which is washed down the dale sides but also to variation in the composition of the limestone itself. Typically on the dale slopes shallow 'rendzina' calcium-rich, alkaline soils develop but leaching can produce a mildly acid, calcium-poor soil. In places, rocky outcrops and scree provide a minimum of soil cover and a very exacting habitat for plants.

The upper plateaux of the Dark Peak are covered with peat and this undecomposed layer of plant material separates plants from the underlying rock. On the higher moors the peat reaches a depth of several metres but over much of the lower moors the peat layer is much less than a metre. The soils produced from the gritstones are acidic and lacking in nutrients. Springs or flushes are common at the junction of shales and gritstones and such areas are often richer in plant species than the surrounding moorland.

In both the White and Dark Peak the soil composition, and factors such as soil moisture content and soil temperature, are strongly influenced by both slope and aspect. In the Dark Peak the distribution of many plants depends on their ability to grow in waterlogged soils and some are restricted to the better-drained, steep slopes. The warmer and drier soils on the south-facing slopes of the limestone dales accumulate less humus than those on the colder and moister north slopes, so not only are growing conditions very different but the soil itself can vary from one side of a dale to the other.

Biotic Factors

The distribution of a particular plant species is also influenced by competition from other plant species, by grazing animals and by the activities of a rather important species—*Homo sapiens*.

Some low-growing plants may be so overshadowed by taller species that they die from lack of sufficient light. Species such as Common Rock-rose (*Helianthemum nummularium*) are commonly found where either grazing, or poor soil conditions keep the growth of taller species in check. Conversely some tall species such as Jacob's Ladder (*Polemonium caeruleum*) will only prosper and successfully flower and seed in the absence of intensive grazing. Some woodland plants such as Wild Arum (*Arum maculatum*) are adapted to growth in low light conditions and may be damaged by too much strong sunlight. Other species such as Spring Cinquefoil (*Potentilla neumanniana*) which is restricted to dry, rocky outcrops exhibits features that enables it to survive drought conditions and grow where few other species can. In other habitats it would be out-competed by faster-growing species, hence its localised distribution.

The results of human activity in the Peak District can be traced back to Neolithic and early Bronze Age times when woodland, thought to have covered most of the area including much of the high moors, was first subject to deforestation. The clearance began in the low altitude limestone regions but then spread to the higher areas and to the woodland cover on the gritstones. In many places regeneration of woodland was suppressed by the grazing activity of agricultural stock (then mostly cattle). Forest clearance continued with the Iron Age settlers and from Roman times onwards woodland was removed to grow arable crops and to provide fuel for lead smelting. In Norman times most of the remaining areas of woodland in the north of the region were included in the High Peak Forest which, like the New Forest, was a Royal hunting area and not a forest in the modern understanding of the word.

Woodland cover in the Dark Peak was influenced both by deforestation and by climate change. As early as 600 BC cooler, wetter weather resulted in an increased washing out of soil nutrients and the growth of heather rather than trees. Peat formation in the areas of higher rainfall, which began some 7,000 years ago, accelerated. As in other parts of the country, woodland on steep valley sides was rarely clear-felled (though it was still actively managed) and among the oldest woods are those in Padley Gorge (on gritstone) and on the slopes of Via Gellia (on limestone).

Archaeological evidence shows that areas of heather moorland were kept clear of trees not only by grazing but also by periodic burning. It is clear that modern heather moorland is not a wild, natural landscape but one that has been created and carefully maintained for the benefit of the chief income providers, namely red grouse and sheep. Grouse require a plentiful supply of young heather to feed on but also older, taller growth in which cover is provided for nesting. The carefully controlled burning of patches of heather (the roots are not killed and the plants sprout new growth from the stem bases) results in nutritious young heather, some of which comes from the establishment of seedlings in the bare earth left after fire. Other areas are left as more leggy, older plants. Where sheep are the main grazers the aim is to produce mostly fresh new growth. Unfortunately accidental fires in dry summer conditions burn much hotter and may not only kill the plants but also burn off the layer of peat thus making recolonisation much more difficult.

Over the last 15 years many of the flower-rich grassland areas of the limestone plateaus and shale regions have been ploughed and reseeded with agricultural cultivars of grasses and clovers. Other meadows are now subjected to weedkiller and fertiliser application. Winter stock feed was previously collected in the form of hay and these hay fields were a rich habitat for a wide range of wild flowers. The introduction of silage, with much earlier cutting of the grass (before many wild flowers have set seed) together with the changes outlined above has greatly reduced the frequency of plants such as Yellow Rattle (*Rhinanthus minor*). Farmers in the Peak District receive grants for the maintenance of flower-rich meadows but this has not prevented the huge loss of such sites in recent years.

Widespread quarrying of the limestone was initiated by the development of coal mining in the Buxton area, the coal provided fuel for use in lime kilns. Much stone was also required for wall building, especially at the time of the Enclosure Acts. Transport has played its part—the coming of the railways (many since closed) facilitated long distance transport, while today much limestone is used for road building as well as in the production of cement. Quarrying often results in unsightly scars on the landscape together with noise, dust and heavy lorries. It can also destroy colonies of some of the rarest plants in the Peak District.

On a more positive side, disused quarries provide a range of habitats such as cliff ledges, quarry floors, scree and spoil mounds and it is here that some of the rarest and most interesting plants of the White Peak are to be found. The absence or paucity of soils, makes the sites less suitable for trees and tall herbs but a species-rich collection of plants develops, especially on the floor and spoil mounds. Included in this collection are a number of orchid species including Fragrant, Pyramidal, Fly and Bee. Some of these are very rare in the Peak District and old quarries provide their principal habitat. Several disused quarries have been designated as Sites of Special Scientific Interest and some have Nature Reserve status.

The Peak District's lead has been extracted by deep mining methods since at least the time of the Romans. The effects of mining on the water table of parts of the limestone plateaux have already been mentioned. The spoil heaps resulting from mining activity represent an extreme environment in which the toxicity of the lead severely limits the growth of many common species. A few species, such as Vernal Sandwort (*Minuartia verna*) are tolerant of lead and are largely restricted to lead-contaminated sites where they are free of competition from other species more susceptible to lead. Some species such as Mountain Pansy (*Viola lutea*) have developed lead-tolerant races, whilst Ling (*Calluna vulgaris*) is able to grow on contaminated spoil heaps because the lead is locked in the fungus associated with that plant's roots. Both *Minuartia* and the much less common *Thlaspi alpestre* were known locally as Leadwort and early prospectors searched for the plants as indicators of where the lead rakes came to the surface.

The coming of the railways produced cuttings (similar to some quarry faces), embankments, and a track-side habitat that was kept clear of tall vegetation by regular cutting and burning. The disused tracks and the spoil mounds associated with their building are home to many native plants including such White Peak rarities as Frog Orchid (*Coeloglossum viride*) and Wintergreen (*Pyrola minor*).

The gritstone quarries of the Dark Peak are less interesting floristically, though they do include some unusual mosses and lichens. Many of the gritstone outcrops are popular climbing routes but, unfortunately, the activities of climbers have helped to remove plant cover. This is an example of the conflicting effects of the many different interests pursued by visitors to the Park and just one more influence on the local distribution of plants in the Peak District.

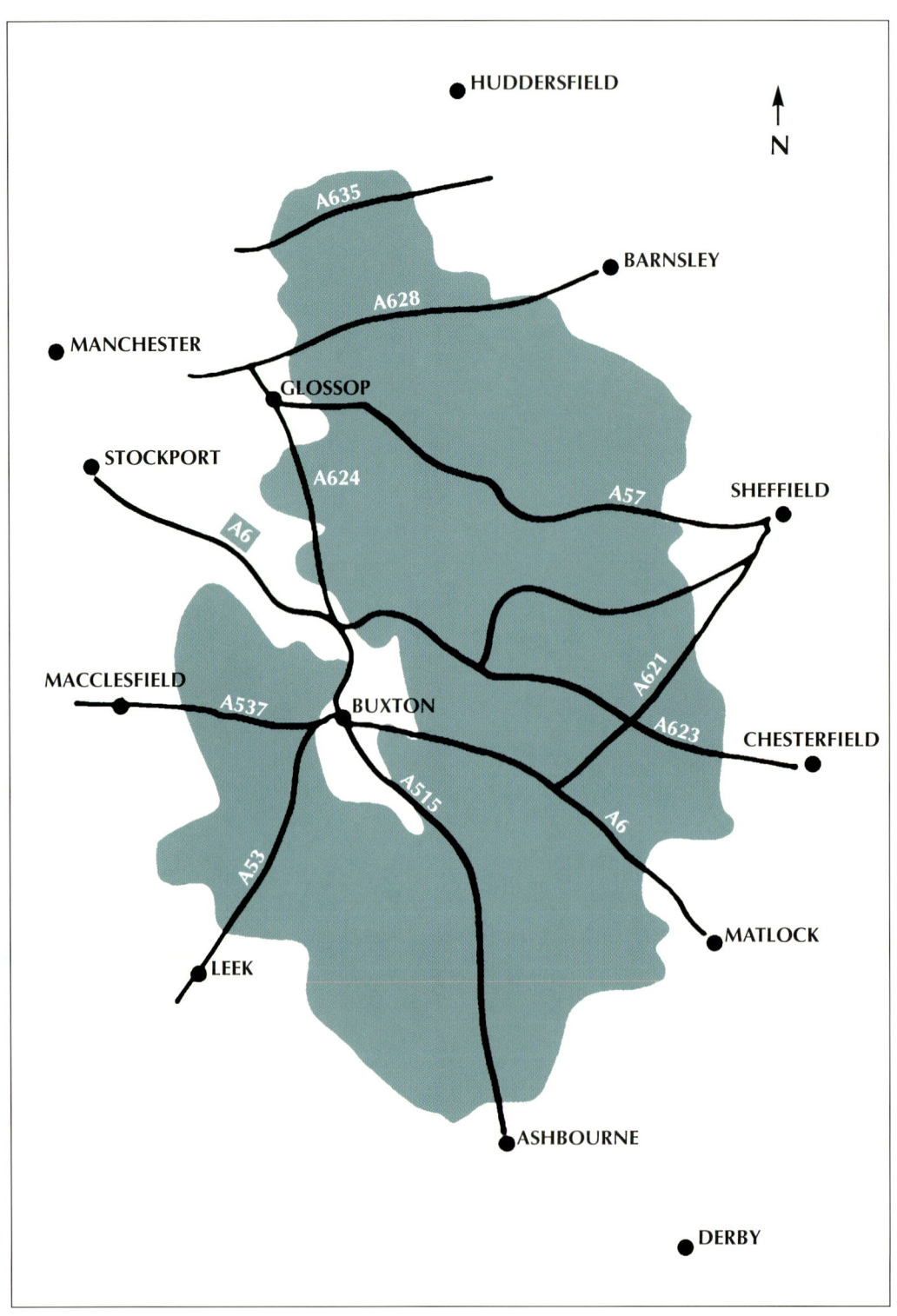

Map showing the Peak District National Park with major towns and cities within easy reach of the Park.

Wild Flowers *of the* Peak District

Green Hellebore	18	Nottingham Catchfly	78
Butterbur	20	Common Rock-rose	80
Lesser Celandine	22	Bird's-foot-trefoil	82
Wood Anemone	24	Kidney Vetch	84
Cuckoo Flower	26	Bitter Vetch	86
Yellow Archangel	28	Yellow Rattle	88
Bluebell	30	Common Spotted Orchid	90
Sweet Cicely	32	Fly Orchid	92
Wild Arum	34	Meadow Cranesbill	94
Bird Cherry	36	Bloody Cranesbill	96
Common Dog Violet	38	Jacob's Ladder	98
Bulbous Buttercup	40	Hoary Plantain	100
Bilberry	42	Fragrant Orchid	102
Cowberry	44	Bee Orchid	104
Ramsons	46	Cross-leaved Heath	106
Cowslip	48	Bell Heather	108
Guelder Rose	50	Cloudberry	110
Wild Strawberry	52	Pyramidal Orchid	112
Gorse	54	Frog Orchid	114
Mountain Ash or Rowan	56	Valerian	116
Toothwort	58	Monkey Flower	118
Lily of the Valley	60	Foxglove	120
Early Purple Orchid	62	Yellow Iris	122
Globe Flower	64	Dyer's Greenweed	124
Columbine	66	Rose-bay Willowherb	126
Mountain Pansy	68	Marjoram	128
Spring Cinquefoil	70	Harebell	130
Water Avens	72	Nettle-leaved Bellflower	132
Meadow Saxifrage	74	Bog Asphodel	134
Ragged Robin	76	Heather or Ling	136

Buttercup Family *Ranunculaceae*

Green Hellebore *Helleborus viridis*

Green Hellebore is a wild relative of the garden plant *Helleborus niger* or Christmas Rose, so-called because its open, rose-like flowers are produced in mid-winter. Both *Helleborus viridis* (from the Latin for green) and the similar Stinking Hellebore (*Helleborus foetidus*) were previously known as Bear's Foot because of their unusual leaf shape.

Green Hellebore is a rare plant in the Peak District where it is close to the northern limit of its distribution. It is probably native though it may have been introduced by Roman or Saxon settlers and some of its current sites probably represent relics of former cultivation. Most sites (e.g. in Bradford Dale and Wormhill) are on limestone, often in or near woodland edges where the plant can be seen flowering from late winter to early spring.

It is a clump-forming, rhizomatous perennial with flowering stems (to 40 cm) which die down in the autumn (*foetidus* to 80 cm and overwintering). Large, long-petioled, dark green, basal leaves have up to 10 toothed leaflets, all arising from one point. Smaller sessile leaves occur on the main stem (*foetidus* has only stem leaves). As the illustration shows the central leaflets are clearly separate but the peripheral ones are connected at the base rather like a bear's toes! There is no disagreeable smell on crushing the foliage as there is with *foetidus*. The saucer-shaped flowers are few (in contrast to *foetidus*), semi-drooping and up to 5 cm across. There are 5 pale-green, petal-like, persistent sepals. In *foetidus*, which occurs as a relic of cultivation in the Peak District, these have a red-purple border, a distinction referred to by Bishop Mant in his poem on the Laws of Nature:

> *What gives the pileworts golden sheen?*
> *The hellebores their blossoms green?*
> *One purple-tipped, the other still*
> *Verdant throughout.*

The 6-12 petals are reduced to tubular nectaries surrounding the numerous stamens (see upper flower in illustration). The fruit (a follicle) is shown developing from a lower flower.

Many *Helleborus* species, hybrids and cultivars are popular in gardens but most have larger, white, cream, pink or purple flowers. Some have been used medicinally and the specific name *niger* comes from the black rhizome which was used (as was that of *viridis*) for its emetic and sedative properties. The plants contain a violent poison, causing diarrhoea and reducing pulse rate in a manner similar to that of Foxglove. Despite having killed grazing cattle the plants were formerly used to worm children and it is interesting that one long-known site for Green Hellebore is the hamlet of Wormhill. The ancient Greeks used Hellebores as a treatment for madness. A tincture from the rhizome is still used homoeopathically in the treatment of epilepsy and some psychoses.

Illustration by
Sheila Stancil

Daisy Family   *Asteraceae* or *Compositae*

Butterbur   *Petasites hybridus*

The Latin name *Petasites* comes from the wide-brimmed sun hat called a petasos. The huge leaves of *Petasites* (the largest of any native British species) are used as parasols, especially by children, but in the Peak District they are more often employed to keep off the rain! The plant grows in or beside water, its common name coming from the former practice of using the leaves to wrap butter which was then immersed in the water to keep it cool. The plant does not produce burs but the leaves are sometimes confused with those of Burdock (*Arctium spp.*) Other names include Wild Rhubarb and Umbrella Leaves.

Butterbur is a plant of streams and riversides (where it is found on alluvial soils) and other damp, shady places. In the Peak District it is locally abundant on the edges (on the banks and also in shallow water) of the Rivers Dove, Wye and Derwent where it often grows under Alder (*Alnus glutinosa*) or Willow (*Salix spp.*) with plants such as Sweet Cicely (*Myrrhis odorata*) and Ramsons (*Allium ursinum*). Unlike most of the rest of Britain where nearly all plants are male (and colonisation is solely from the breaking up of the underground rhizome) female plants, producing masses of feathery seeds, are common in parts of the Peak.

In a manner similar to Coltsfoot (*Tussilago farfara*) Butterbur is unusual in that it flowers before the leaves expand fully. As early as March the compact flowering stem bursts through the soil like a purple-pink mushroom. The terminal portion bears large numbers of stalked, composite flower-heads, each surrounded at the base by a number of purple, sepal-like bracts. The stem base is covered in overlapping pink-veined bracts which occasionally end in tiny green leaf blades (see illustration). On male plants the flower-heads are on short stalks and contain many tiny tubular flowers with stamens surrounding a club-shaped, sterile stigma. To add to the confusion there may also be some sterile, ray-like female flowers. The female plants produce flower-heads on longer stalks (which like the main flowering stem elongate as the seeds are produced—see left side of illustration) with a forked stigma protruding from each flower. Some of the central flowers may be sterile males!

The seeds are dispersed by a parachute of long white hairs. The basal leaves emerge (beside the flowering stems) in late March and carry on growing all summer. The blades, with their grey, felty undersides, can reach a metre across and are borne on very long, grooved petioles.

Illustration by Jacqueline Dawson

Buttercup Family *Ranunculaceae*

Lesser Celandine *Ranunculus ficaria*

This beautiful little plant is blessed with a strange collection of names. Celandine comes from 'chelidon' the Greek word for a swallow and the belief (according to Pliny) that swallows used the plant juice to improve the eyesight of their young. Lesser Celandine, or Spring Messenger as it was also called, flowers from February onwards, well before swallows arrive and it is probable that the plant of the fable is the non-related Greater Celandine (*Chelidonium majus*) which flowers from May. The specific name *ficaria* comes from the Roman 'ficus' meaning fig and refers to the elongated fig-shape of the root tubers. It was once known as figwurt and in 1548 William Turner in his book *Names of Herbs* wrote 'Figwurt groweth under the shadowes of ashe trees'. This was at the time it was used to treat 'fig' now known as piles (the swellings of which are fig-shaped). Figwurt has become Pilewort and is still used by herbalists today.

Lesser Celandine is common and widespread throughout the Peak in woods, damp pasture, by water and by paths, especially on valley bottoms. The fleshy, glossy leaves emerge as early as January. They have a scalloped edge and are often freckled with silver or bronze. The burnished yellow, pointed petals which vary in number from 7–12 (typically 8) close at night and in dull weather, and finally fade to almost white. The undersides are greeny-brown. The petals are surrounded by just 3 green sepals, which fall as the flower matures. The open flower is pollinated by bees and flies. The fruit, of small green nutlets, resembles that of a Buttercup.

Ranunculus ficaria occurs in two forms. Subspecies *bulbilifera* (formerly known as *bulbifera*) sets little fertile seed but spreads from its bulbils that form in the leaf axils after flowering. Confusingly, a bulbil in this case is not a little bulb but a small, above ground, root tuber. Subspecies *ficaria* spreads from seed and does not produce bulbils. Celandine seedlings are unusual in that they possess only one seed leaf (cotyledon) but they are still classed under the major division of the flowering plants known as the Dicotyledons!

Lesser Celandine grows as a weed in some gardens but a number of cultivars are sold as garden plants by nurseries; these include 'Double Bronze' and also 'Collarette' where the stamen filaments are like small leaves. As a wild plant it was beloved by Wordsworth who wrote three poems about it (including *To a Small Celandine*) and there is a carving of it on his tomb in Grasmere. Sadly this appears to be Greater Celandine so confusion between the two plants continues!

Illustration by Cyril Stocks

Buttercup Family *Ranunculaceae*

Wood Anemone *Anemone nemorosa*

The word Anemone comes from the Latin for 'windy place' hence the alternative name Windflower but *nemorosa* refers to a 'woodland glade' not really a windy habitat. In Greek mythology Anemones were said to spring from the tears of Aphrodite. A less attractive name for this plant was Smell Fox, a reference to the rather rank smell of the flowers, but in Derbyshire the shape of the closed flower is alluded to in the old local name of Moggie-nightgown.

Anemone is common in Peak woods and hedgerows and also in grassland that was previously wooded but it is less frequent on the more acid soils of the Dark Peak. It is early to flower, typically from March to late May in the Peak. It is a normally glabrous perennial (up to 30 cm) and its long-stalked, deeply cut 3-lobed leaves arise from a slender, brown, underground rhizome.

The usually solitary flowers are 2–4 cm across and only open in full sunshine. During dull weather and at night the closed head droops gracefully. Some two-thirds of the way up the flower stem are three lobed leaves that fold over and protect the flower bud, other long-petioled leaves arise from the rhizome. Wood Anemone is often confused with Wood Sorrel (*Oxalis acetosella*) a spring flowering plant of similar habitats but this smaller plant has Clover-like leaves and flowers with 5 small green sepals and 5 lilac-veined white petals. In contrast Wood Anemone has no true petals but 5–9 sepals which look like petals. These are normally white but often contain shades of pink or purple, especially on their outer surfaces (see photograph).

A number of cultivars are grown in gardens including 'Robinsonia' with larger, pale lavender-blue flowers and 'Virescens' in which tiny leaves replace the sepals and stamens. There are also double-flowered forms.

In common with other members of the Buttercup family the plant contains chemicals which cause blistering and irritate the digestive tract. Animals usually ignore it but there have been poisonings, mostly in the spring. It is not used in herbal medicine but it has been used homoeopathically as a 'cure-all'.

Wood Anemone can survive in deep shade for many years without flowering. Removal of shade, such as by tree felling or coppicing, results in a dramatic increase in flowering. The seeds however are not widely dispersed and are often infertile. Vegetative reproduction by way of the rhizome is effective but the rate of spread may be as little as 2 metres in 100 years. The lack of colonising ability frequently limits Wood Anemone to current or past sites of Ancient Woodland; that is woodland that was in existence before AD 1700.

Illustration by Cyril Stocks

Cabbage Family   *Brassicaceae* or *Cruciferae*

Cuckoo Flower   *Cardamine pratensis*

This plant is blessed with a multitude of common names. In many parts of the country the flowers emerge just as the cuckoo arrives but the plant often harbours cuckoo spit, the froth-like protection of young frog-hoppers, and so was previously called Cuckoo Spit in parts of northern England. Other popular names include Lady's Smock, and Milk Maids—the latter from its association with damp grassland where the pink flowers were 'enjoyed by milk maids'. The link with maids could be more of a sexual one—Cuckoo being a derivative of cuckold, while an alternative 16th-century meaning of the word smock was slang, equivalent to 'a piece of skirt'. An old Derbyshire name was Lucy Locket, which puts a very different perspective on the nursery rhyme!

Cuckoo Flower is a plant of poorly drained grassland, from road and stream sides to damp pasture and moorland flushes. This is a similar habitat to that of Ragged Robin (see page 76). It is more common on lowland areas of the Dark Peak but also grows on north-facing limestone grassland. It does not compete well with taller plants and is thus helped by light grazing. Like Ragged Robin its frequency has declined significantly in the last 30 years.

Cuckoo Flower is a perennial with little-branched, glabrous flowering stems to 50 cm. The dark green, basal rosette leaves are long-stalked with pairs of rounded leaflets and a larger, kidney-shaped terminal one. The margins are sparsely toothed. The stem leaves are short-stalked, with a greater number of much narrower leaflets. There are 4 small, mauve-tipped green sepals and 4 lilac or pink, notched petals that are only occasionally white—as in Shakespeare's line in Love's Labour's Lost 'lady-smocks all silver white'. Each flower contains 4 long-stalked and 2 short-stalked yellow anthers and a central, club-shaped stigma. The slender upright fruit pods split open with such force that seeds are ejected up to 2 metres from the plant.

Small plantlets develop where leaflets touch damp soil. When leaves or pieces of stem become detached they too are capable of producing new plants. This vegetative reproduction is probably more important than spread by seedlings in many sites. The double-flowered garden cultivar 'Flore Pleno' was collected from the wild where it occurs as a rare mutation. It is sterile but readily produces new plantlets from its basal leaves.

Cuckoo Flower is an important food plant for the caterpillars of the Orange Tip butterfly. The female (without the orange wing tips and looking more like a small Cabbage White) lays her eggs among the developing flower buds.

Illustration by Irene Mackerness

Mint Family *Lamiaceae* or *Labiatae*

Yellow Archangel *Lamiastrum galeobdolon*

In the Middle Ages those plants (such as this one) that looked like nettle but did not sting were grouped under the name Archangelus. Today such species include Red and White Deadnettle and Yellow Archangel. Its former Latin name was *Galeobdolon* (meaning 'weasel' and 'a bad smell') *luteum* (meaning yellow). The weasel feature refers to the flower shape—the plant being called Weasel Snout in some areas. The bad smell is emitted when the leaves or stem are crushed. It was also called *Lamium galeobdolon* but members of the genus *Lamium* (including the Deadnettles) have pubescent anthers and other features that separate them from the new genus *Lamiastrum*.

Yellow Archangel is found in many of the older woodlands and shaded hedgebanks of the Peak District, especially on moist soil that is not too acidic. It is early flowering and often associated with other vernal species such as Wood Anemone (*Anemone nemorosa*) Wild Arum (*Arum maculatum*) and Ramsons (*Allium ursinum*). Dense shade suppresses flowering but it forms large patches from its rooting runners (see illustration). It has poor long distance dispersal which probably accounts for its virtual absence from new woodland.

Lamiastrum is a perennial which sends up unbranched, slightly hairy, square-sectioned stems (to a height of 40 cm) from horizontal, surface runners. The light-green, opposite, nettle-like leaves have margins with irregular, coarse teeth. Leaves on new runners (which emerge after flowering) are more broadly oval in shape. Flowers are produced in stalkless whorls from the leaf axils. The green, softly hairy, calyx tube ends in 5 pointed teeth. The corolla forms a tube (up to 2 cm long) ending in two lips, the upper yellow and helmet-shaped; the lower three-lobed with dark red markings (see illustration). The 4 anthers are hairless. The persistent calyx surrounds the fruit of four green nutlets.

In the 1960s Variegated Yellow Archangel (subspecies *argentatum*) appeared, probably having arisen as a garden mutation. Unlike some variegated forms of the wild type, this has permanent conspicuous silver-white blotches on the upper leaf surfaces and is very invasive by virtue of its long runners and the fact that it is ignored by slugs! It is now widely cultivated and dumped garden thinnings have become naturalised in places such as roadside verges and woods not colonised by the native form.

Illustration by Cyril Stocks

Lily Family *Liliaceae*

Bluebell *Hyacinthoides non-scripta*

Bluebell is a plant of the moister parts of western Europe and is at its most abundant in Britain. Other, older names include Cuckoo's Stockings, Wild Hyacinth and Harebell but Bluebell is now almost universally accepted. The Latin name has also seen changes, such that within the last 20 years it has been included in two other genera: *Scilla* and *Endymion*. The mythical Hyacinth of ancient Greece was said to have had AIAI (alas) inscribed on its petals by Apollo following the death of Prince Hyacinthus. Our Hyacinth-like plant is without such markings, hence *non-scripta*.

In the Peak District, Bluebell is locally common in broad-leaved woodland on all but the most acid soils and also grows on the site of former woodland. It even occurs in some conifer plantations and with Bracken (it finishes flowering before the fronds unfold). Research has shown that picking the flowers is not in itself detrimental but grazing and trampling is. Damaged leaves are not replaced, the number produced each year being predetermined. Since 1998 it has been illegal (even with the landowner's permission) to uproot wild Bluebell bulbs. This follows years of habitat destruction by illicit suppliers of bulbs to garden centres.

Bluebell is a perennial showing early growth from a small (2–3 cm) bulb that is renewed each year. The glossy, linear leaves (up to 40 cm long but only 2 cm wide) are keeled and have a hooded tip enabling them to push through leaf litter. All leaves are basal. The slim, leafless flower-stem bends at its apex and bears a one-sided head of nodding (but erect in bud) strongly-scented flowers, each on a short stalk with a pair of blue bracts at its base. The blue (or lilac or white) tepals form a narrow, parallel-sided tube with 6 reflexed lobes at the apex. The anthers are cream-coloured. Naturalised plants of the Garden, or Spanish Bluebell (*Hyacinthoides hispanica*) and hybrids with our native species can be distinguished by their wider leaves and less-scented flowers which stick out at right-angles all round the stouter, erect stem. The more open flowers have blue anthers.

In earlier times starch, for stiffening clothes, was extracted from the bulbs (see also Wild Arum page 36). Bad luck was said to come to those placing Bluebells in the living room. Chemicals in the poisonous bulb are currently being investigated as potential treatments for both HIV and cancer—the plant beloved by poets may yet prove to have a more practical beauty.

Illustration by Penni Ravenhill

Carrot family *Apiaceae* or *Umbelliferae*

Sweet Cicely *Myrrhis odorata*

Like the biblical Myrrh this plant is very aromatic, with a smell of liquorice or aniseed, and is sometimes known as Anise. It contains an essential oil (anethol) which is used in the flavouring of Chartreuse. Dioscorides wrote about the medicinal virtues of a similar plant known as 'Seseli' and this is the likely derivation of the English name. Sweet Cicely was commonly grown as a garden herb and the leaves and fruits are still used to flavour apple pies and to remove the sharpness from cooked rhubarb. It is not now regarded as a native species but as a long-naturalised garden escape.

In the Peak District, as elsewhere, *Myrrhis* grows on road verges close to farms and old houses. It is also locally common in much more natural-looking sites and on shady river-banks (for example by the Rivers Derwent and Wye) where it may form dense stands along with natives such as Butterbur (*Petasites hybridus*). The large fruits are water dispersed and the plant does not readily colonise drier sites. Except on the acid gritstones it is much more common in the Peak than it is further south and is one of the first of its family to flower (as early as March).

Sweet Cicely is a perennial herb with a short tap root and rather fern-like, compound leaves (it is sometimes called Sweet Bracken). The large pale-green leaves are softly hairy and the segments near the main leaf stalk are frequently marked with white blotches. This feature, together with the aniseed smell, distinguishes it from another early flowering relative, Cow Parsley (*Anthriscus sylvestris*). The terminal flower-heads are borne on stalks (like umbrella spokes) at the end of erect, green, hollow stems (up to a metre tall). Stem leaves have a sheathing base marked with longitudinal veins. Each tiny individual flower contains 5 white petals, often unequal in length and with incurled, pointed tips. Not all flowers contain both functional male and female organs.

The huge, erect, laterally flattened fruits are up to 2.5 cms in length. They are deeply ridged and retain the forked, beak-like stigma at the narrow apex. Initially green (see illustration) they ripen a dark shiny brown. In addition to the previously mentioned culinary use, their oil content has been used to polish wood. The plant is used by herbalists as a carminative and diuretic and has also been employed to lower blood pressure.

Illustration by Trudy Roe

Arum Family *Araceae*

Wild Arum *Arum maculatum*

The unusual appearance of this plant when in flower has attracted almost 100 different common names, most with a sexual connotation. Lords and Ladies is one of the more polite ones and Cuckoo Pint (to rhyme with mint) is a cleaned up version of Cuckold's Pintle—the latter term being slang for a penis. More vulgar names include Bulls and Cows and the highly descriptive Dog's Dick. Even the apparently innocent Wake Robin is probably more to do with the sexual antics of Robin Goodfellow, rather than the activities of a bird. The Latin *maculatum* refers to purple-black spots on the leaves but in the Peak the majority of plants (over 75 per cent), like the one illustrated, have unblemished leaves.

Wild Arum is most common in the shade of woods, hedges and walls on the more fertile but well-drained soils in the Peak District. As a vernal (spring-flowering) species it is often found together with Dog's Mercury (*Mercurialis perennis*) and Yellow Archangel (*Lamiastrum galeobdolon*). The poisonous leaves are rarely grazed.

Arum maculatum over-winters as an underground, starchy tuber from which the leaves emerge in February and March. The glossy leaf blades are triangular or arrow-shaped in outline though some (see left of illustration) are more rounded. Unlike most other species of Monocotyledon they do not have parallel veins. The long petioles overlap at the base from where the round-stalked, cowl-like spathe emerges from mid April onwards. The spathe is paler than the leaves and is often suffused with purple. The lower part wraps round (in some plants left over right, in others right over left) to form a chamber from which the finger-like spadix emerges. This is normally dark purple but about 5 per cent of the Peak District plants have a pale-yellow spadix. Chemical reactions in the spadix produce heat and a smell that attracts owl-midges into the chamber so ensuring cross-pollination. The upper flowers consist of red-brown stamens, below these are whorls of ovaries (like Corn on the Cob). By late summer the leaves, spathe and spadix wither, leaving the poisonous orange-red berries at the stalk apex.

The tubers were an early source of starch for the laundry industry (one wonders if Robin Starch packets should picture Wake Robin rather than the bird) and in the early 19th century they were baked and ground to provide Portland sago, a substitute for arrowroot. The plant is used in homoeopathy to treat gastritis, spotted plants being deemed the more efficacious.

Illustration by Judy Pickles

Rose Family *Rosaceae*

Bird Cherry *Prunus padus*

In the Peak District, Bird Cherry largely takes the place of Wild Cherry (*Prunus avium*) which is more frequent further south. In 1597 Gerard called it the Bird's Cherry Tree and the bitter fruits have long been regarded as fit only for the birds. At this point it would be nice to record that Bird Cherry was called *Prunus avium* but the Latin link with birds has become associated with Wild Cherry—much to the confusion of many budding botanists! Other local names include Hagberry and Heckberry.

In the Peak District, which is close to the south eastern limit of this small tree in Britain, it is usually found in moist, shady sites such as river banks, north-facing slopes and as an understorey shrub in woodlands. It occasionally occurs in the oak woods of the Dark Peak (especially in locally waterlogged soils on shale) but is more common in the White Peak where it occurs particularly in the valley bottoms and is indicative of older woodland. It is often associated with shrubs such as Dogwood (*Cornus sanguinea*) and Guelder Rose (*Viburnum opulus*).

Bird Cherry is a small, bushy, deciduous tree, which rarely tops 15 metres. The bitter-smelling brown bark peels off in strips and is dotted with elongated orange lenticels (breathing pores). The glossy-brown shoots bear alternate, thin, elliptical leaves edged with pointed teeth. The blades are smooth but for hair tufts in the vein axils below. At the blade end of the petiole are a pair of glands (see illustration). Unlike Wild Cherry, which bears flowers and fruits in small hanging clusters, Bird Cherry produces up to 40 almond-scented flowers (in May) on an arching flower spike. Each small (under 2 cm) flower has 5 free, white petals with jagged edges. There are numerous stamens. The small (less than 1 cm) ovoid fleshy fruits ripen a shiny black but lack the sweetness of cultivated cherries.

The bark has been used as a sedative in homoeopathic medicine and for the treatment of bronchitis and whooping cough by herbalists. The tree was formerly much planted in central and southern England where it has become naturalised. As a garden plant it is most frequently represented by the cultivar 'Watereri' which has fewer, larger leaves and an even longer spike of flowers. The introduced Laurel (or to give it its full name, Cherry Laurel—*Prunus laurocerasus*) is a close relative with similar flower-spikes and shiny black berries but the large, leathery leaves are evergreen.

Illustration by Shelley Jones

Violet Family *Violaceae*

Common Dog Violet *Viola riviniana*

John Gerard is reputed to have translated the Latin name for what we now call Heath Violet (*Viola canina*) as Dog Violet. Several species of violet now include dog as part of their name and as they all lack a scent, the popular name (as explained by the herbalist Mrs Grieve), is 'a reproach for the want of perfume'. Other derogatory plant names include Horse Chestnut (not the edible one) and Toadflax (no use for making linen).

Common Dog Violet is frequent throughout the Peak District, especially in woods and limestone pasture (where it often grows with Common Rock-rose—see page 80) but it also grows on the more acid moorland grasslands of the Dark Peak. It flowers from late April to June which is later than the Early Dog Violet (*Viola reichenbachiana*). Plants from very exposed sites often have smaller leaves and flowers and were formerly regarded as a subspecies though they are now classed as *Viola riviniana* variety *minor*.

Viola riviniana has a central, non-flowering rosette of leaves (see illustration) which is absent in Heath Violet. The long-petioled, heart-shaped, typically glabrous leaves are only slightly longer than broad (they are more elongated in Heath Violet) and are edged with rounded teeth. Two narrow, toothed stipules arise from the stem end of the petiole. Flowers are borne from side shoots, on curving stalks. The 5, pointed green sepals have obvious appendages which project towards the stalk and enlarge in fruit. (Early Dog Violet has only tiny appendages). The 5 broad, blue-violet petals overlap (they don't in Early Dog Violet) while the rear-facing, broad spur is much paler (often cream) and furrowed at the tip. The tapering, unfurrowed spur of the Early Dog Violet is the same colour as the rest of the flower.

The early, showy flowers are insect pollinated but research has shown that they generate less seed than from the smaller flowers produced later in the year. These cleistogamous flowers don't open and are self-pollinated. The fruit capsule splits into three, flinging out the seeds. Dispersal is further aided by ants. New plants also arise from the roots.

The related Sweet Violet (*Viola odorata*) differs in being downy, with rooting runners and having deep violet or white flowers with less-pointed sepals and a sweet scent. It is found mostly in the White Peak, often close to gardens. Extracts of this plant have long been used for cosmetic and medicinal purposes.

Illustration by Margaret Wightman

Buttercup Family *Ranunculaceae*

Bulbous Buttercup *Ranunculus bulbosus*

The Latin *Ranunculus* appears to be associated with the fact that many species of Buttercup grow in water or on damp ground, the same habitat as the frog (*Rana* in Latin). Most of these moisture-loving plants are white-flowered and are now classed as species of Water-Crowfoot while yellow-flowered species are known as Buttercups, a term which did not come in until the late 18th century. This species was formerly known as Bulbous Crowfoot despite being a plant of well-drained soil! The well-hidden bulbous part is the swollen, corm-like stem base (see lower right illustration).

It is common, especially in the White Peak, where it flowers from early May on the drier, shallow-soiled, grazed pastures, dale sides, old limestone quarries and lead spoil heaps. In these habitats it takes the place of the much taller and later-flowering Meadow Buttercup (*Ranunculus acris*). Buttercup petals are frequently used in the wonderful floral pictures that are created as part of the ancient Peak District custom of well dressing.

Apart from the bulbous stem base, *bulbosus* differs from the more moisture-loving Creeping Buttercup (*Ranunculus repens*) by not producing creeping runners, and from *R. acris* by being less than 40 cm tall and having less-dissected leaves. It is the only common species of Buttercup in which the sepals, having protected the bud, turn down as the flower matures and the many stamens release their pollen. Each yellow petal (there are usually 5 but the number can vary) secretes nectar from near its base which helps to attract insect pollinators. The fruit is a cluster of small, flattened, green nutlets (achenes).

Bulbous Buttercup is suppressed by taller vegetation and so benefits from grazing animals which also create the bare soil areas essential for seedling establishment. The thin limestone soils it grows on are very prone to summer drought and the leaves and flowers normally die down to the swollen stem base by mid-July thus enabling the plant to pass the dry season in a dormant state.

Grazing animals rarely eat species of *Ranunculus* as they contain chemicals that cause mouth blisters and digestive disorders. Despite this, many children's books depict a cow happily munching Buttercups—a very false picture, as was the belief that very yellow butter came from cows fed on Buttercups. As for a Buttercup under the chin to test a liking for butter, I can report that it doesn't work with beards! Buttercups were used in the 16th century in an attempt to combat plague sores and are still used homoeopathically to treat skin ailments such as eczema.

Illustration by Chrissie Vale

Heath Family *Ericaceae*

Bilberry *Vaccinium myrtillus*

This plant has a host of common names throughout Britain but Bilberry is the most frequently used in this area. A name used in parts of Yorkshire is Blaeberry, meaning blue-black berry. Some local people refer to the fruits as whorts and the plant as Whortleberry. The berries are not only rich in vitamins C and D but also contain a lot of tannin which is why they were used (raw) as a treatment for diarrhoea. In the latter half of the 19th century (before the days of a long summer holiday) school children from Eyam were excused lessons in order that they could gather Bilberries for the local chemist. They are still gathered as food by those (myself included) who value their tartness but it takes dedication and hard work to collect a sufficient quantity!

Bilberry is locally frequent on the moorlands (where the berries are eaten by grouse) and in open woodland on the millstone grit. It also occurs on some of the shale soils but is only rarely found on limestone. In some areas it has been eliminated by the spread of Bracken and where it is found in open woodland it usually produces fewer flowers in the shadier conditions. It is more tolerant than Heather of heavy grazing by sheep and can exist as a very low-growing plant. Experimental plots (fenced to keep out grazing animals, as those at the top of Padley Gorge) produced a hundred-fold increase in the height of the Bilberry plants!

Bilberry is a small, hairless, deciduous shrub with an extensive creeping rhizome from which vegetative spread occurs. In shaded conditions and where grazing animals are restricted it can reach a metre high but is generally less than half this in exposed sites. The green, angled stems enable the plants to photosynthesise before the new leaves emerge. The pale green, mat, ovate leaves have a fine-toothed margin. The usually solitary, pendant flowers are produced over a long season (from April to August) and are topped by a dome-like calyx of small green sepals. The five pale-pink, waxy petals are fused into a bell shape from which the style protrudes. The green globular fruits (up to 1 cm across) ripen a deep blue-black, with a slight grey bloom.

Cowberry (*Vaccinium vitis-idaea*) is a close relative and is illustrated on page 45. Where the two species co-habit and overlap for part of their flowering periods, as they do in a few places to the west of Sheffield and in the western Peak (Staffordshire) they hybridise to produce *Vaccinium × intermedium*. This is intermediate in all its characters and such plants will occasionally set seed.

Illustration by Catherine Zurbrugg and Jean Binney

Heath Family *Ericaceae*

Cowberry *Vaccinium vitis-idaea*

This plant is much less well-known than its close relative the Bilberry, with which it often grows. It differs from Bilberry in having red rather than blue-black fruits and is also known as Red Whortleberry. For the same reason it is also known as Cranberry but the true Cranberry (*Vaccinium oxycoccus*) which occurs infrequently in the Peak District, is a tiny prostrate plant with miniature Cyclamen-like flowers. The cow part of the name may have come from the Latin 'vacca' meaning a cow though some authorities believe that vacca is a corruption of 'bacca' meaning berry. Given the barely edible nature of the fruit (though it is used in so-called Cranberry Jam) it may be another example of an animal part of a plant name indicating a lack of use. The specific *vitis-idaea* is said to come from Mount Ida (now spelled Idhi) in central Crete. An old Yorkshire name was Flowering Box, a reference to the similarity of its leaves with that of Box (*Buxus sempervirens*).

In the Peak District, Cowberry is at the southern edge of its distribution in Britain where it is a plant of northern uplands. It is rarely found below 200 metres but its waxy leaves make it very drought resistant and it is most common in the Peak District on south-facing slopes. Like Bilberry, its rhizome is susceptible to water-logged conditions but it is more tolerant of grazing (the leaves are less palatable) and of burning. A plant of well-drained slopes and cliff ledges on the higher moorlands of the Dark Peak it is still found in a few White Peak sites as a relic of the former heathland.

Cowberry is a low-growing, evergreen shrub with a creeping rhizome. Unlike Bilberry the twigs are not angled and the leathery leaves are very dark green and glossy above but present a net-like appearance from the glands on the paler under-surface. The edges are turned under and not obviously toothed. The leaf apex is not pointed and may be slightly notched. Flowering is later than Bilberry, typically not beginning until June, with drooping clusters of 3–4 pinky-white, waxy bell-shaped flowers at the stem apices. At the wide-mouthed apex of each flower are 5 turned-back lobes. The firm, globular, red fruits are up to 1 cm across and are normally in groups of 2 or 3. The berries have a sharp taste.

As mentioned in the description of Bilberry, there are a few areas in the Peak District where Cowberry and Bilberry hybridise, a fact first noticed in 1870, but the number of sites where this occurs is very limited.

Illustration by Jill Holcombe

Lily Family *Liliaceae*

Ramsons *Allium ursinum*

Ramsons (frequently misspelled Ransoms) comes from 'hramsan' which is Old English for Wild Garlics (the singular is 'hramsa' so 'Ramsons' is a double plural!) In parts of the Staffordshire Peak District it was known as Ramshorns and while this may be due to the twisted leaf stalk it is probably just a derivation of Ramsons. It is also known as Wild or Bear's Garlic, the Latin *ursinum* means 'to do with bears'. Some say this comes from the leaf shape being like a bear's ear, others from the belief that the plant was eaten by bears. It is also likely that the animal link is a derogatory one in that Ramsons is not such a useful culinary plant as are its close relatives, onion and garlic.

Ramsons forms large patches in moist, shady places and in the Peak District it is most common under trees fringing streams and rivers, where rich soil is deposited during periods of flooding. It is more frequent on the lime-rich soils of the White Peak. It is a vernal species and is very evident (both visually and by its powerful onion smell) in late April and May, along with other spring flowers such as Wood Anemone (*Anemone nemorosa*) and Yellow Archangel (*Lamiastrum galeobdolon*) but by July most of its leaves have died away and many summer visitors to the Peak are unaware of its existence. It is not a good coloniser of new sites and is thus more likely to be found in more long-established woodland.

Each plant produces 2 or 3 large, basal, elliptical-oval, bright-green, hairless leaves with parallel veins on the blade, and a long, narrow petiole, which is twisted through 180 degrees. The thicker leaves of Lily of the Valley (see page 60) are a similar shape but lack the strong onion smell which is very noticeable when the leaves of Ramsons are bruised. Below ground is a small bulb consisting of just one leaf base. The flowers (from 5 to 20 in number) radiate from the end of an unbranched, leafless, stalk which is triangular (or semi-circular) in cross-section. Just below the flower-head are two papery bracts which enfold the buds. Each flower has 6 long, pointed, spreading tepals and 6 narrow-stalked orange stamens.

Ramsons does not produce the bulbils of Garlic or the large bulbs of Onion but the leaves make a fine addition to a salad and contain the same health-promoting disulphide chemicals. This was neatly summarised in the 17th century proverb:

> *Eat leekes in Lide (March) and*
> *ransoms in May*
> *And all the yeare after physitians may play*

Dairy farmers are less pleased if the plant is eaten by cows as this can taint the taste of both their milk and butter.

Illustration by Chrissie Vale

Primrose family *Primulaceae*

Cowslip *Primula veris*

Cowslip is an unattractive name for such a beautiful flower—slip was a word meaning wet dung and the plant was said to grow wherever a cow pat (or slip or slop) had fallen. Other common names on the same theme include Carslope and Cow Strupple. The plant with its head of drooping flowers was said to have sprung from the place where St Peter dropped the keys to heaven, hence the name Bunch of Keys. Milton wrote 'Cowslips wan that hang the pensive head' and the nodding flowers were used by herbalists in the treatment of paralysis, resulting in the old name Palsywort. Some books still include the common name Paigle (or Paigles) which is probably a derivation of the word paralysis.

Nationally, Cowslip numbers declined sharply from the 1950s as a result of the ploughing up of old pasture and also because of the use of chemical sprays on road verges. The decline was less marked in the Peak where it is still locally common especially among short grass and in scrub and open woods in the limestone dales. The sight of thousands of yellow and orange Cowslips growing with Early Purple Orchids on the dale slopes from late April to June is enjoyed by walkers and botanists alike. Cowslip is also found away from limestone but does not occur on the wet acid soils typical of much of the Dark Peak.

Cowslip is a perennial with winter green leaves produced as a basal rosette and in the more heavily grazed dales these are pressed closely to the ground. The dark green, almost hairless leaves have a wrinkled appearance and the blade narrows abruptly to the petiole, which often carries a wing of green on each side (see leaf in lower left of illustration). The erect flower stem bears no leaves, just a terminal head of 10–30 nodding flowers, the stalks of which all come from the same point. The 5 green sepals are fused for most of their length and from them emerges a tube formed by the 5 joined, yellow petals which spread to a funnel-shape at its apex. The yellow is spotted with deep orange in the throat of the flower. The apricot-scented flowers have either a short style, below the stamens (thrum-eyed) or a long style reaching the throat (pin-eyed). The fruit stalks stand erect.

The False Oxslip, a hybrid between Cowslip and Primrose is not uncommon where the two parents grow together in the Peak, such hybrids were the origin of some of the Polyanthus group of cultivated Primulas. The hybrid holds its flowers upright, unlike the true Oxlip (*Primula elatior*) which is not found in the Peak District.

Illustration by Judy Pickles

Honeysuckle Family *Caprifoliaceae*

Guelder Rose *Viburnum opulus*

This attractive shrub is not related to the Rose but is in the same family as Elder (*Sambucus nigra*). Indeed an earlier name for this plant, which is usually found on damp soils, was Water Elder. John Gerard, famous for his *Herbal* of 1597, knew it as Rose Elder or Gelder Rose. It is most well known as the popular garden cultivar 'Roseum' which is often called the Snowball Tree and was introduced from Holland in the 16th century. To be precise it came from the Dutch province then known as Guelders which led to the native plant also taking the Guelder epithet. An old Yorkshire name was Dog-tree, possibly a derogatory name for a plant without much use (unlike Elder that was much used medicinally and for making dyes) or because it was used for making 'dogs' (wooden skewers) for meat.

Guelder Rose is often overlooked when not in flower or fruit but is in fact frequent on moister soils in both the White and Dark Peak. It grows in woods as part of the understorey and is most common in the White Peak under Ash *(Fraxinus excelsior)* but also grows with Hazel (*Corylus avellana*) scrub. It is found in some of the Oak (*Quercus petraea*) woods of the Dark Peak.

Viburnum opulus is a deciduous shrub that rarely exceeds 3 metres in height. Its much-branched stem produces slightly angled, smooth, grey twigs bearing many-scaled buds. The leaves, like those of the Maple genus that they resemble, are borne in opposite pairs. The blade is normally 3 (rarely 5) lobed, up to 8 cm across and with an irregularly toothed margin. The petiole bears small glands and there are two small finger-like stipules at its base (see illustration). The dark green leaves turn red-purple in autumn.

Flowering is in June and July when flat-topped, circular flowerheads are formed. In the centre of the head are many tiny (6 mm across) tubular white flowers containing 5 stamens and 3 stigmas. Round the edge of the head are much larger (to 20 mm) more flattened, 5-lobed flowers. The showy outer flowers serve to attract insect pollinators (they are said to smell like well-peppered, fried trout!) but are in fact sterile. The inner flowers produce a cluster of spherical, fleshy, scarlet fruits that look as if they have been varnished.

The garden cultivar 'Roseum' has a domed flowerhead consisting entirely of the more showy sterile flowers and is often mistaken for a species of *Hydrangea*. As it only produces sterile flowers it does not form fruit and is propagated vegetatively.

Illustration by Judy Pickles

Rose family *Rosaceae*

Wild Strawberry *Fragaria vesca*

Many people believe that Wild Strawberry was the species from which large-fruiting cultivars were developed, in fact the commercially grown plant is a hybrid between two American species (*Fragaria × ananassa*) which was introduced into Britain, from France, in the 18th century. So-called Alpine Strawberries, grown in gardens, are in fact cultivars of Wild Strawberry. It is frequently stated that the name relates to the practice of putting straw round the plants but the term Strawberry predates the use of straw to lift the fruits clear of the ground; the Anglo-Saxon word 'streowberie' referring to the runners (stolons) that were strewn over the ground. The Latin *Fragaria* is a reminder of the rich fragrance of the ripe fruit.

In the Peak District, Wild Strawberry is most commonly found on limestone soils where it grows under the partial shade of Ash–Hazel scrub and in disturbed woodland. In 1603 Ben Jonson wrote 'A pot of Strawberries gathered in the wood to mingle with your cream'. If the shade is too intense it produces fewer flowers and seeds but still spreads by its rooting runners. It also grows in open sites such as scree slopes, disused limestone quarries and on the beds of old railway tracks. It is able to grow on poor soil where competition from taller-growing plants is less intense.

Wild Strawberry is a perennial with a woody base from which arise long stolons that root and produce new plants. The long-petioled trifoliate, bright green leaves are finely pubescent on the upper surface (*ananassa* is hairless) but paler with appressed hairs below. The margin is edged with even-sized, large teeth. The leaves are often confused with those of Barren Strawberry (*Potentilla sterilis*) but this has blue-green leaflets with spreading hairs on both sides and uneven-sized marginal teeth. Clusters of flowers are borne on leafless stems. The 5 green sepals are surrounded by similar-looking bracts which are just visible between the broad, often overlapping, petals (in Barren Strawberry the petals are more spaced). The fleshy green fruit, which ripens red when the sepals spread or turn back, can be up to 2 cm across and has seeds (achenes) projecting from its surface. (Barren Strawberry has a cluster of dry achenes and no fleshy fruit.) Naturalised Garden Strawberries may have similar-sized small fruits but the sepals envelop the fruit-base.

Fruits of Wild Strawberries are rich in vitamin C and have long been collected and even sold in markets. The leaves and roots contain tannin and were used medicinally for the treatment of diarrhoea, in contrast to the fruits which act as a mild laxative.

Illustration by Jacqueline Dawson

Pea Family *Fabaceae* or *Leguminosae*

Gorse *Ulex europaeus*

There are many common names as alternatives to Gorse (from the old English 'gorst' meaning waste) including Furze and Whin. In parts of Derbyshire it was known as Ling, a term more generally used for Heather (*Calluna vulgaris*). There are two common species of Gorse in Britain: *europaeus*, which is the most widely distributed and *gallii* (Western Gorse) which has a more westerly distribution. The Peak District is close to the eastern limit of *gallii* and where it occurs it is often in the cloughs of the Dark Peak, in the most acid moorland or on the few remaining patches of limestone heathland.

Gorse rarely dominates the landscape in the Peak and is mostly found in patches of rough, moderately acid pasture (pH 4–6), avoiding both very acid and also calcium-rich soils. It does occur in the White Peak but mostly on deeper (calcium-free) soils. The old saying 'when the Furze is out of bloom, kissing is out of season' is a licence for romance as one or other species of Gorse is in flower for almost the whole year; *europaeus* mostly from January to June, and *gallii* mainly from July to November—Mistletoe helps fill the gap in December! Gorse flowers have a strong scent, variously described as being like coconut or vanilla. The petals used to be added to the cooking water to add colour to boiled egg shells at Easter.

Ulex europaeus forms a bush, up to 2 metres in height, bearing rigid, dark-green, branched spines (the true leaves are reduced to scales). The spines are deeply grooved (*gallii* has less-rigid, shallowly-grooved spines and is a smaller plant) and the golden-yellow flowers are up to 2 cm long (*gallii* flowers are a lighter yellow and smaller). The explosive (and audible) splitting of the hairy pods which dry in the sun, flings out the small pea-like seeds that are further distributed by ants. The hard seed coat can survive high temperatures and Gorse seedlings often appear after fire. Seedlings have trifoliate, clover-like leaves but these are soon replaced by spines. The deep tap-root enables established plants to regenerate after fire.

Young shoots of Gorse were fed to cattle and horses in the winter, after first crushing the spiny branches. Gorse twigs were used for sweeping chimneys and for making besoms and the dried branches made excellent kindling for bakers' ovens and lime-kilns. The flowers are still used for making wine, though, in contrast to the similar but non-spiny Broom, the plant has rarely been used medicinally. Gorse is not a popular garden plant (pruning can be a painful experience) but there are a few cultivars such as the double-flowered 'Flore Pleno'.

Illustration by Nancy Brockington

Rose Family   *Rosaceae*

Mountain Ash or Rowan   *Sorbus aucuparia*

The genus *Sorbus* includes other trees such as Whitebeam and Wild Service Tree. Mountain Ash has been recorded growing at an altitude of over 900 metres, higher than any other British native tree species, and it does have an Ash-like leaf. In the Peak District it is more commonly called Rowan, this name is associated with rune and the old Norse alphabet said to have been carved on its bark. It is also known locally as Quicken and this is probably linked to it being a tree of protection, one that endows life, as in the term 'quick and the dead'. It was sometimes planted in churchyards to prevent the dead from rising! Rowan was more often planted near houses, its wood being deemed especially efficacious as a protection against witchcraft.

Rowan is frequent throughout the Peak District as it grows on a wide range of soil types but it is much more common on the moist, acid soils of the Dark Peak. It is found in woodland (especially the Oak woods of the Dark Peak but also in some of the limestone dale woods), scrub and especially by streamsides and on rocky moorland sites, including cliff ledges. It is even found in some conifer plantations.

Sorbus aucuparia is a small, short-lived, deciduous tree with a smooth grey-purple bark. Older twigs are also smooth but young twigs are downy. The large purple-brown leaf buds have an incurved tip. The compound leaves are borne alternately, unlike those of Ash (*Fraxinus excelsior*), and typically consist of 6 or 7 pairs of sessile, oblong, pointed leaflets and a stalked terminal one. All leaflets have a regular, saw-toothed margin. The leaves are dark-green and smooth above, grey and downy below. In autumn, the leaves of Rowan trees in the Peak turn vivid shades of orange and red, a much more pronounced colour change than that seen in trees further south.

Large flat-topped flowerheads are produced in May and June. The clusters of strong-scented flowers are initially erect but later arch over. Each small flower (c. 1 cm across) has 5 green sepals and 5 creamy-white petals. Typical of the Rose family there are many stamens. The hanging clusters of 1–2 seeded, globose berries ripen in late summer from green through yellow and orange to scarlet. 5 lines at the end of each berry (see illustration) remind us of the pentagram symbol, possibly one reason for the plant's supposedly magical powers.

In the past, the berries were used as bait to trap birds by fowlers, and also to mitigate the effects of scurvy. They are still used to make a jelly to accompany meat dishes. Rowan is a popular choice for roadside planting schemes and a number of cultivars are grown in gardens including 'Fructo Luteo' with yellow berries. Similar, non-native species are also widely planted.

Illustration by Pauline Snaith

Broomrape family *Orobanchaceae*

Toothwort *Lathraea squamaria*

This strange looking plant contains no chlorophyll and as a result has no green colour, even in its reduced, scale-like leaves. It is a parasite that does not make its own organic food, as all green plants do, instead it steals nutrients from the roots of certain tree species. The only part of the plant visible is the inflorescence which looks like a straight set of dentures. Both the scale-like leaves and fruit capsules are reminiscent of teeth, but the plant was also known as Corpse-flower as it was formerly believed by some that this rather ghostly looking plant grew out of a buried corpse!

Toothwort is not common in the Peak District but is most frequent in the White Peak especially on damp soil in woods and old hedgerows. It is associated with a number of trees and most records are with Hazel (*Corylus avellana*) though it also occurs with Elm (*Ulmus glabra*) and Alder (*Alnus glutinosa*). It is probably under-recorded as it is only evident above ground for a few months and it is well camouflaged against a backdrop of dead leaves and twigs.

Toothwort is a perennial with a branching rhizome covered with overlapping, fleshy white scales. In April and May the stout aerial flower-stems are produced. These are initially pendent at the tip but later erect and up to 25 cm tall. They occur in clusters close to the host tree. The base of each stem is covered in cream-coloured scales (the specific name, squamaria, means scaly). The spike of flowers is one-sided (this helps distinguish Toothwort from similar-looking species of Broomrape) and each short-stalked flower is borne from the axil of a scale.

The hairy calyx is cup-shaped with 4 equal-sized, triangular lobes at its apex. The petals, which are white or a delicate purple-pink, are fused into a two-lipped corolla. The upper lip encloses the 4 stamens, the lower lip is weakly 3-lobed. A club-shaped stigma protrudes from the corolla. The corolla soon fades and turns brown, at which point the ivory-white, shiny capsules develop.

Toothwort is recorded as having been used as a cure for toothache (this being an example of the belief held in earlier centuries that the shape or colour of a plant was a clue as to its medicinal virtues) but it was not widely used, no doubt because of its rather ethereal nature.

Illustration by Cyril Stocks

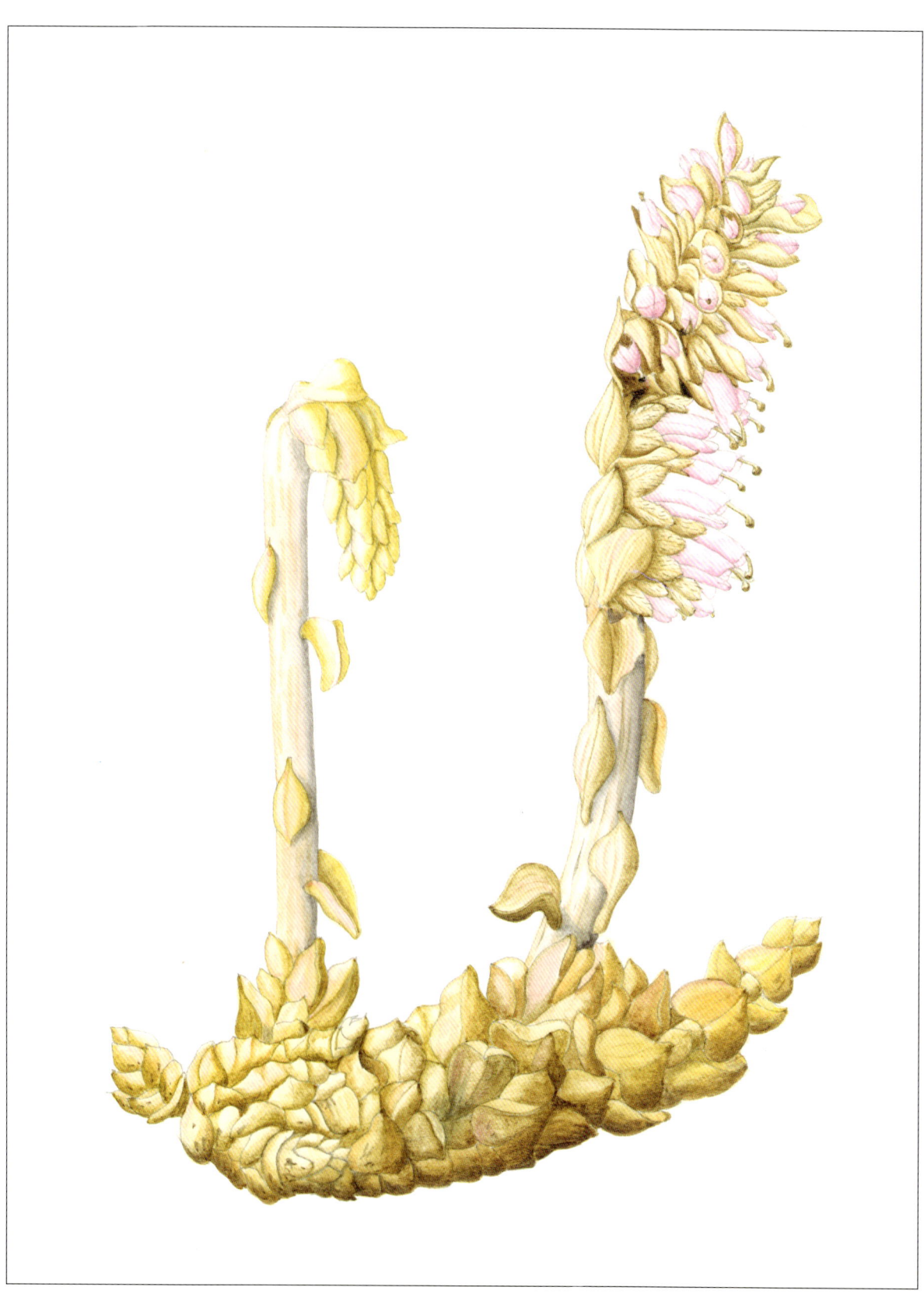

Lily Family *Liliaceae*

Lily of the Valley *Convallaria majalis*

'Lilium convallium' mentioned in the biblical Song of Solomon, is most likely to be a species of *Hyacinthus* which grows in the Middle East. Convallium comes from a Latin word meaning a dell or valley and it is possible that Lily of the Valley is a corruption of the old biblical name. The specific *majalis* indicates 'belonging to May' and it is also known as May Lily. In more southern parts of Europe its fragrance is associated with May Day but under the Gregorian calendar it rarely starts to flower before the middle of May in the Peak District. (May 1st would now be about two weeks later if we had not abandoned the Julian calendar in 1752).

In the south and east of England *Convallaria* is found on sandy soils but in the Peak District it is a plant of the limestone where it is largely confined to old woods and Hazel scrub vegetation on the site of former woodland. Many of the White Peak's more ancient woods are on the steep dale slopes which are unsuitable for farming. Lily of the Valley is still locally frequent under Ash, Hazel and Oak on the thin soils, and scree slopes, of places such as Monsal Head, Ravensdale and the Manifold Valley. On many of these sites other rarities can be found such as Nettle-leaved Bellflower (*Campanula trachelium*) and Herb Paris (*Paris quadrifolia*).

Lily of the Valley forms large patches from a branched, far-creeping underground rhizome (see illustration). The leaves can be confused with those of Ramsons (see page 46) but lack the strong smell of onion. Two (or rarely three) smooth, parallel-veined, oval-elliptical leaf blades (up to 20 cm long) are borne on long sheathing petioles. Below these are several purple-veined scale-like bracts. The leafless flowering stem arises from the axil of one of these bracts and bears up to a dozen, sweet-smelling flowers, all drooping to one side. Each bell-shaped flower is made up of 6 thick, fused white tepals (3 sepals and 3 petals all similar). The 6 terminal lobes bend outwards. The red-currant like fruits are rarely produced in the wild, which is one reason for the plant's poor ability to colonise new sites.

Lily of the Valley is poisonous and has long been regarded as an omen of ill-luck if brought into the house, its scent, however, is still widely imitated in soaps and perfumes. The plant contains two glycoside chemicals which have a powerful effect on the heart muscles and in the past it was used medicinally as a substitute for Foxglove (see page 120). It has long been grown in gardens and there are a number of cultivars one of which, 'Hardwick Hall', has pale green margins to its very broad leaves.

Illustration by Sylvia Ford

Orchid Family *Orchidaceae*

Early-purple Orchid *Orchis mascula*

This is the earliest flowering wild orchid, hence the name Early-purple (and also a former Yorkshire name Cuckoo Flower—now widely used for *Cardamine pratensis* which also flowers early). Of the many former local names some, such as Cross-flower, drew attention to the leaves, said to have been splashed with the blood of Christ but most, like the Latin name, are associated with the two underground tubers—*Orchis* being the Latin for testicle. For centuries the newly filling, firm tuber was used as an aphrodisiac (the older, more wrinkled one was used to dampen desire!) and was the main constituent of love potions. Before the introduction of coffee, the starchy tubers were made into a 'health drink' known as salep.

Early-purple Orchid is a plant of base-rich soils (it will not prosper on acid soils). In southern England it occurs most frequently in shady woods and hedgebanks where it grows with other spring flowers such as Bluebell. In the Peak District it is a striking component of the limestone dales where it is locally abundant on the grassy slopes and limestone ledges. Flowering reaches its peak in mid May, some weeks before any other species of orchid comes into flower in the Peak District.

Orchis mascula has swollen, unforked tubers and a rosette of spirally arranged, long, narrow, dark-green shiny leaves. These and the sheathing stem-leaves are broadest above the middle and are marked with purple blotches (elongated along the leaf). Parts of the solid stem are often suffused with purple (see illustration). The young inflorescence is enclosed in a sheathing leaf. Purple-mauve flowers are widely spaced up the stem and have an unpleasant (tom-cat) smell which is stronger at night. 2 lateral sepals (petal-like) spread out while the rear sepal and 2 of the petals curl inwards. The larger front lip is 3-lobed and usually paler in the centre where there are a few purple spots but the rest of the flower is of a uniform colour (in contrast to the Spotted Orchids, see page 90). A long, blunt-ended spur sticks out behind the back of the flower.

Victorian books call it Early-purple Orchis, the term orchis coming from the Latin for the genus. The word orchid is much easier to pluralise and gradually replaced orchis during the 20th century—a reminder that plant names are constantly evolving.

Illustration by Anne Dent

Buttercup Family *Ranunculaceae*

Globe Flower *Trollius europaeus*

This plant is found throughout much of northern Europe but has nothing to do with trolls! The Latin name is more likely to have come from the old German word 'troll' meaning rolled in. This referred to the flower shape, whose globe-like outline was recorded by Gerard in 1597. An early name 'Gowan' meant simply a yellow flower and this was also used for Daisy (with its yellow centre). An old Yorkshire name for *Trollius* was Cabbage Daisy—the plant with a cabbage-shaped, yellow flower.

Globe Flower is not common in the Peak District, which is at the south-eastern edge of its distribution in Britain. In fact most of its sites in the area are in moist pastures, under open woodland or Hazel scrub, on north or west facing slopes of the limestone dales. It flowers in June and July together with other tall herbs such as Valerian, Meadow Cranesbill, and Jacob's Ladder, all of which feature in this book. Most of its sites are in the Wye Valley and are being closely monitored. If the local climate is becoming warmer and rainfall patterns are changing (as a result of global warming?) *Trollius* may become extinct in the Peak as it withdraws to the cooler and damper north.

Globe Flower has erect, little-branched stems to 70 cm high, arising from a stout, perennial stock. Basal leaves have 5 palmate lobes, deeply toothed margins and long petioles. Stem leaves are mostly sessile and much smaller. All leaves are glabrous unlike the similar-shaped leaves of Meadow Cranesbill (see page 94). The large, terminal, pale-yellow/green flowers are up to 4 cm across. The outer parts consists of some 5–15 overlapping, incurved yellow sepals which look like petals. Hidden inside are a similar number of strap-shaped, nectar-secreting petals and a mass of stamens. The dry fruits bear distinctive transverse wrinkles.

Globe Flower grows well beside garden ponds and in shady borders. Cultivars of our native species include 'Canary Bird'. Other related garden plants include introduced species and those of a hybrid origin. Over-collection of our native species to stock Victorian gardens probably contributed to its current rare status. In common with other members of the Buttercup family, Globe Flower contains a range of poisonous chemicals but has been little used medicinally.

Illustration by Sylvia Ford

Buttercup Family *Ranunculaceae*

Columbine *Aquilegia vulgaris*

Both the Latin and English names of this attractive plant relate to the strange flower shape. Each petal ends in a nectar-secreting spur, the knobbed tip of which is likened to an eagle's claw—'aquila' is Latin for eagle. Each spurred petal looks like a dove—the Latin 'columbae' means a cluster of doves. Similarly, the old name Culverwort probably came from the Saxon word 'culfre' meaning a pigeon. Granny's Bonnet is a name reflecting the hat-like appearance of some of the older garden cultivars in which the flowers have shorter spurs.

Columbine is infrequent as a wild plant but is found (mostly in the White Peak) in woods, scrub and on some shaded dale sides (for example in Deep Dale) where the blue (occasionally purple, pink or white) flowers appear from May to early August. As early as 1629 Parkinson remarked on the many varieties that were being grown in gardens and it has remained a popular garden plant. Modern cultivars include white ('Nivea'), flesh and two-toned flower colours, with many, such as 'Nora Barlow,' having double flowers. Some represent hybrids with other species. Most grow from seed very easily and often become naturalised on road verges and near habitation.

Aquilegia vulgaris is an erect perennial with a branched, red-purple stem up to a metre high. Long-stalked basal, pale or blue-green leaves are typically divided into three lobes, each of which is further divided into three. Upper leaves are sessile, with a blade of three narrow lobes. All leaves are softly downy on the underside. 5 petal-like sepals alternate with the spurred petals on a drooping flower stalk which straightens as the cluster of hooked fruits develop. The hay-scented flower is pollinated by insects, such as bees, that have a tongue long enough to reach the end of the nectar-containing spurs. The fruit is like a hand of erect fingers. The seeds are black and shiny.

The plant is poisonous and while it is mentioned in Culpeper's herbal of the 17th century it is no longer used medicinally in Britain. In the Middle Ages it was held that Columbine rubbed on the hands would give one the courage of a lion. It is depicted among the carvings of Ripon cathedral and in a beautiful 16th-century painting by Durer. Later, the plant was regarded as an emblem of worthlessness, in 1605 Chapman wrote 'What's that? A columbine? No! That thankless flower grows not in my garden'. Shakespeare mentions it in several plays, in Hamlet (Act iv scene 5) it is gathered by Ophelia as a symbol of ingratitude to her faithless lover.

Illustration by Valerie Oxley

Violet Family *Violaceae*

Mountain Pansy *Viola lutea*

Pansy comes from the French word for the plant, 'Pensée' (meaning a thought). Pansies have long been a favourite in literature, Wordsworth wrote of 'The Pansy at my feet' and Shakespeare (Ophelia) 'There's pansies, that's for thoughts'. It was not until last century that the term became slang for a male homosexual, possibly as a corruption of the earlier term 'nancy'. *Viola lutea* is absent from lowland England, hence the Mountain epithet but it does grow at lower altitudes in Scotland. The specific name *lutea* means golden yellow and this adequately describes the flower colour of most of the plants found in the Peak though a minority are purple-flowered (see lower illustration).

Mountain Pansy has a patchy distribution in the Peak District. It occurs in neutral or slightly acidic, short grassland on shale and more especially on the soils which are found where rain has leached out the calcium on the upper dale slopes in the White Peak. Grazing keeps down taller plants which would otherwise shade it out. Unlike most plants, Mountain Pansy can tolerate high levels of lead and frequently occurs on the old spoil heaps associated with the lead rakes. Vernal Sandwort, known locally as Leadwort (*Minuartia verna*) and the little Moonwort fern (*Botrychium lunaria*) also occur on lead-contaminated soil where lack of competition from species susceptible to lead allows these tolerant species to flourish.

Viola lutea is a low-growing perennial, spreading from a slender rhizome. The toothed leaves become progressively narrower higher up the stem. There is a pair of deeply-lobed stipules near the petiole base. The large (up to 3.5 cm long) terminal flowers appear from early May and are borne on slender stalks. Each of the 5 pointed, green sepals bears a toothed appendage at its base (see flower bud in the upper illustration). Of the 5, usually yellow, petals, the lowest is the broadest and ends in a spur some 2-3 times the length of the sepal appendages (see left hand flower in the upper illustration). This petal retains a yellow base even in purple flowers and is delicately lined with violet veins.

The closely related Wild Pansy (*Viola tricolor*) is very rare in the Peak District. It lacks the rhizome (it is often an annual) and has slightly smaller flowers, typically with a mix of three colours: purple, pink and yellow. The flower spur is only a little longer than the sepal appendages. The two species occasionally hybridise and such hybrids were the origin of many of our Garden Pansies or Violas, which are usually annuals or biennials and have much larger flowers than those of the wild parents. There are numerous Viola cultivars exhibiting a huge range of flower colour.

Illustration by Sue James

Rose family *Rosaceae*

Spring Cinquefoil *Potentilla neumanniana*

The genus name *Potentilla* means 'a little powerful one' a name linked to the extensive medicinal use made of species such as Silverweed (*Potentilla anserina*) and the supposedly magic power (as a talisman against witchcraft) of some of the more common Cinquefoils. The 5-fingered leaf (hence the name Cinquefoil), is depicted amongst the carvings in the chapter-house of Southwell Minster. Spring Cinquefoil was originally given the Latin name of *Potentilla verna* as it is vernal, or spring, flowering. This was later changed to *Potentilla tabernaemontani*, in honour of the artist Jacob Theodore who illustrated the plant in 1590. His Latinised name 'Tabernaemontanus' (tavern on a hill) was taken from his home town. Now the plant is called *Potentilla neumanniana*; it would seem that some Latin names are nearly as ephemeral as the common ones!

Spring Cinquefoil is a rare plant that has been present in the Peak District since post-glacial times (over 10,000 years ago.) It grows on limestone outcrops, mostly on the top edges and usually on south-facing slopes—one such well-known site is on the south side of Cheedale. It rarely spreads far from an outcrop as it is easily shaded out by taller growing species. Plants growing in isolated sites are less likely to be cross-pollinated and research has indicated that some Peak populations produce seed without the male (pollen) genes. This results in the plants of a small area being very similar but differing in leaf shape (or other features) from plants a few miles away.

It is a prostrate, mat-forming perennial, with woody stolons which root at the branch points and are covered in old brown stipules. Basal leaves have long petioles and 5–7 palmate, toothed leaflets (see illustration). Flowering stems bear short-petioled leaves with fewer leaflets. At the base of each leaf petiole is a pair of narrow, pointed stipules. In May and June flowers (to 15 mm across) which open in sunshine, are produced on hairy stalks. The 5 green sepals are surrounded by small green sepal-like bracts (see flower in illustration, top right). The 5 yellow petals are notched at the apex and are slightly longer than the sepals.

Both *Potentilla neumanniana* and the closely related *Potentilla crantzii* (Alpine Cinquefoil) are grown in rock gardens. The latter has larger, more orange-yellow flowers, broader stipules and is not mat-forming. Garden cultivars of Spring Cinquefoil include 'Goldrausch' and 'Nana'—both produce more flowers than the wild type.

Illustration by Ivy Brown

Rose Family   *Rosaceae*

Water Avens   *Geum rivale*

The genus *Geum* takes its name from a Greek word meaning 'yielding an agreeable flavour' and one of its commonest species, *Geum urbanum* (Wood Avens) has a clove-like taste to its roots. An association with brooks is the translation of 'rivale' but, in northern Britain, the plant is not restricted to stream-sides and river valleys as the name implies. It is absent from the moorlands but is otherwise not infrequent in the Peak District, especially by water but also in damp woodland margins and among long grassland on north-facing slopes (and shady railway cuttings) of the limestone dales. It usually grows in more open conditions than the aptly named Wood Avens.

Water Avens is a softly hairy perennial with flowering shoots up to 50 cm. Long-petioled basal leaves bear small, different-sized, pairs of toothed leaflets and a larger, more rounded, terminal lobe (see illustration). Leaves on the flowering stems are much smaller, virtually sessile and 3-lobed. All leaves have a pair of small (less than 1 cm) green stipules at their base. The nodding flowers (up to 2 cm across) are borne singly or in small clusters. The 5 long sepals and surrounding narrower bracts are dark-red or purple. Each broad, purple-veined, orange-pink petal, narrows suddenly near its base.

The 5 petals form a deep cup surrounding the many stamens and styles. After the petals drop off, the stalk straightens and the fruit head develops as a mass of achenes, each with a hook at the end of a long style. The bur-like fruits are distributed by animals, including birds.

In parts of the Peak, especially in some of the wooded limestone dales, *Geum × intermedium*, the hybrid between Water and Wood Avens occurs, along with both parents. Wood Avens differs in that the terminal section of the basal leaves is tri-lobed and the leaves have longer stipules. The smaller, erect flowers have 5 green sepals and 5 yellow petals (not abruptly narrowed at the base) which open flat. Hybrids exhibit a mix of the parental characters and are unusual in that they are highly fertile and may backcross with the parents. It has been speculated that habitat disturbance (farming, woodland management etc.) may have brought these two species together and facilitated the production of hybrids.

Water Avens grows well in gardens where it is found as cultivars such as 'Coppertone' and 'Lemon Drops' but these are often pollinated by nearby plants of Wood Avens and so are not easy to keep pure. Most other related garden plants are cultivars of non-native species such as *Geum chiloense* and *Geum coccineum*.

Illustration by Jean Binney

Saxifrage Family *Saxifragaceae*

Meadow Saxifrage *Saxifraga granulata*

Most of the Saxifrages grow on rock or amongst stones, indeed it was once thought that they had the power to split rock hence the name *Saxifraga* meaning 'rock breaker'. This species has granular, pea-sized bulbils among the upper roots hence its specific name. Many plants found on rocky soil were previously used in herbal medicine for the treatment of stones in the kidney and bladder. In fact this species is found in grassland but the kidney-shaped lower leaves may have drawn the attention of herbalists under the Doctrine of Signatures, where features such as plant shape or colour provided clues as to its use. In 1597, Gerard recorded that the seed (actually the bulbils) of what he called White Saxifrage made good medicine for the bladder and kidney.

In the Peak District, Meadow Saxifrage grows in moist limestone pastures where it is still locally abundant, especially in valley bottoms and on some of the deeper soils. It also occurs on slightly acidic soils on the shales and millstone grit. It was previously a component of the hay fields but the change to silage has eliminated it from such habitats. It has been present in the area since early post-glacial times along with rarer species such as Jacob's Ladder (see page 98).

Meadow Saxifrage forms a basal rosette of sticky, sparsely hairy leaves (these are often hidden in the grassland sward). Each has a long petiole and a blade that is rounded or kidney-shape in outline, with a margin of 7–10 blunt, rounded lobes. Just below ground, in the axils of the older leaves, are clusters of red-brown bulbils. The erect (to 50 cm) flowering stem is covered with hairs and those in the upper region are glandular and sticky. Upper stem leaves are few and very different, with a shorter petiole and narrower, more pointed lobes. Open clusters of Buttercup-size flowers are produced from May to early July. 5 green sepals are united at the base and covered in glandular hairs. Inside the 5 creamy-white petals are 10 stamens, 5 of which shed their pollen before the other 5. The persistent styles give a horned appearance to the fruit, a two-sectioned capsule. The plant dies down by August and becomes dormant until new leaves appear in the following spring.

Meadow Saxifrage was originally grown in gardens as a medicinal plant but is now grown for its graceful flowers. Cultivar 'Plena' has double flowers. Fingered Saxifrage (*Saxifraga tridactylites*), a tiny annual of limestone outcrops and walls, is locally common but rarely seen by the Peak's many summer visitors as it has set seed and died by August. The rarer Mossy Saxifrage or Dovedale Moss (*Saxifraga hypnoides*) is local in the dales where it forms mats of small, moss-like leaves on scree and rocky limestone grassland.

Illustration by Trudy Roe

Pink Family *Caryophyllaceae*

Ragged Robin *Lychnis flos-cuculi*

The scientific name for this plant, with its bright coloured flowers, comes from the Greek word lychos meaning 'a lamp'. The specific *flos-cuculi* means 'flower of the cuckoo'—an older English name was Cuckoo-flower, a name now usually reserved for Lady's Smock or *Cardamine pratensis* which like *Lychnis* flowers as the cuckoo arrives. The 'ragged' part of the English name is an apt description of the deeply cleft petals but 'robin' is more open to argument! Some say that the flower is the colour of a robin's breast, others that the plant was associated with St Rudbert which became Rupert and finally Robin. Even the house goblin figure of Robin Goodfellow may be implicated. The older name, Wild William, reminds us that it is in the same family as the cultivated Sweet William.

Ragged Robin is a plant of damp meadows and marshes on poorly drained soils and is more common at lower altitudes than those found in much of the Peak District. Here it is most at home on some of the wet flushes in the moorland regions. It has become less common in Britain over the last 40 years, partly as a consequence of the improved drainage of agricultural land.

It is an erect perennial (to 75 cm) that is hairless but has a rough feel. The entire-margined leaves are borne in opposite pairs. Those at the base of the flowering stem and on non-flowering side shoots have long blades (up to 10 cm) and a petiole; others are smaller, more slender and clasp the stem. Clusters of flowers form at the ends of the branching stem in early summer. 5 dark-green sepals, with 10 purple-red veins, are united into a tube with 5 teeth at its apex. The 5 much longer petals are fused at their bases but separate and bend flat once clear of the sepals. Each spreading petal is deeply cut into 4 narrow lobes that spread out like fingers, there are also two forked, scale-like lobes at the petal base. The petals are a rich rose-red or purple-pink (occasionally white). Each flower is up to 4 cm across and includes 10 stamens and 5 styles, unlike the related Red Campion, *Silene dioica*, in which the neater flowers contain either stamens or styles but not both. The fruit is a dry brown capsule.

Gerard pointed out that the plants were not used in medicine but 'they serve for garlands and crowns and to decke up our gardens'. It is still grown in gardens where it is popular beside ponds. Cultivars include one with white flowers and a low-growing dwarf form. Ragged Robin is closely related to the popular garden plant from south-eastern Europe known as Rose Campion—*Lychnis coronaria*.

Illustration by Jan Relton

Pink Family *Caryophyllaceae*

Nottingham Catchfly *Silene nutans*

In 1671, Thomas Willisel who was Britain's first professional plant collector, took the famous naturalist John Ray on a tour of northern England. One of the places they visited was Nottingham castle, the first recorded site for *Silene nutans*, but sadly it disappeared from the castle during restoration work in the 19th century. The name Catchfly may have arisen from the fact that small insects get caught among the sticky hairs of the plant but it is also pollinated by flies and by night-flying moths (see inset photograph).

Silene nutans is a rare plant of dry rocky places on the south coast (chalk cliffs), in north Wales and in Scotland. It is more widely distributed in the Peak District than anywhere else in Britain and is still locally common on, and at the edges of, south-facing limestone outcrops as in Miller's Dale and also in Dovedale and its tributaries. It is often associated with plants such as Marjoram (*Origanum vulgare*) and Bloody Cranesbill (*Geranium sanguineum*).

Nottingham Catchfly is like a straggly White Campion (*Silene latifolia*). It has short non-flowering shoots and long, erect flowering ones (up to 75 cm). The softly hairy stem becomes increasingly sticky in the upper regions. The leaves are also softly hairy, in opposite pairs: the basal ones broad and stalked, stem ones narrow and virtually sessile. Flower stalks arise from the upper leaf axils and each head contains 3–7 drooping flowers (*nutans* is the Latin for nodding). The 5 sticky, green and purple-veined sepals form a tube from which the 5, deeply cleft, white petals emerge. There are 10 stamens and 3 styles. Leaf width and flower colour vary in different populations (the plant illustrated has yellow patches near the petal ends which is not uncommon).

Flowering in June and July the flower development follows an interesting sequence. In the late afternoon the filaments of 5 stamens elongate thus projecting their anthers from the still unfurling petals (see lowest flower in illustration). By nightfall pollen is shed, as is a sweet scent which attracts night-flying insects. The following evening the other 5 anthers release their pollen (see highest flower in illustration). By the third evening the anthers have all withered and the petal ends have turned back. At this point the 3 styles elongate and the stigmas become receptive to pollen (see third flower down in illustration). This unusual pattern of events ensures that the flowers are cross pollinated—but it also means they are at their best in dull evening light which does not make it easy for the illustrator!

Illustration by Mary Acton

Rock-rose Family *Cistaceae*

Common Rock-rose *Helianthemum nummularium*

The yellow flowers of this plant only open when the sun shines, helio is the Greek word for sun, and it was formerly known as Sunflower (the name we now give to *Helianthus annuus*). As Mediterranean species of Rock-rose, in the closely related genus *Cistus*, were introduced to our gardens in the 16th century, Gerard called our native plant 'English Yellow Dwarffe Cistus'. Unlike introduced species it rarely reaches above 30 cm high and an earlier Latin name was *Helianthemum chamaecistus*, meaning low-growing *Cistus*.

Rock-rose has been present in the Peak since late Glacial times and is frequent as a species in the short turf grassland of the limestone regions. It grows in well-drained, grazed pasture, on scree slopes and rocky outcrops and even on lead mine spoil along with plants such as Mountain Pansy (see page 68). These habitats often become very dry in summer but Rock-rose has a long tap root (see illustration) the ability to shed its leaves under severe drought conditions, and leaves with hairs on the underside which help reduce water loss.

Helianthemum is like a tiny shrub with branches arising from a woody base. The small, narrow, oblong, evergreen leaves are mostly paired except for those just below the flowers. The leaves have untoothed, slightly down-rolled margins and are covered in white woolly hairs below. At the base of each petiole is a pair of narrow, pointed stipules. The saucer-shaped flowers on drooping stalks are grouped in loose clusters and are produced from early June until late August. They vary in size from 1–2 cm across. Each flower has two outer, narrow green sepals and three larger inner ones (see right hand flower in illustration). The 5, bright yellow, petals sometimes have an orange spot at their base and are initially crinkled, as if made of tissue paper—a feature more pronounced in species of *Cistus*.

The numerous orange stamens attract bees and other insects. During poor weather, when the flower closes, pollen is pushed onto the style and self-pollination occurs. The fruit is a rounded capsule surrounded by the sepals. Long-range seed dispersal is not very effective and Rock-rose is not good at establishing on new sites—one reason why it has become rarer under the more intensive management of pasture in lowland England. The sprawling branches often take root where they touch the ground, resulting in vegetative reproduction and spread within a site.

Many of the garden Rock-roses are non-native species but some are cultivars of *nummularium*. The root is rich in tannin and was formerly used for its astringent properties and also as a vulnerary in herbal medicine. It is the source of one of the Bach Flower Remedies being used for people suffering from acute fear or panic.

Illustration by Ivy Brown

Pea Family *Fabaceae* or *Leguminosae*

Bird's-foot-trefoil Lotus corniculatus

This common plant has acquired at least 70 English names, many highlighting different features of the plant. Even the Latin name is open to interpretation as *corniculatus* may refer to the curved, horn-like flower buds or come from 'cornicula' meaning a little crow. The horizontally held, divergent seed-pods create the image of a bird's foot. Lady's Fingers and the cheekier Grandmother's Toenails are names in the same vein. The contrasting colours of the buds and flowers gave rise to the name Eggs and Bacon, or Eggs and Collop as it was known in parts of northern England. Another local name was Lady's Slipper, from the resemblance of the flower shape to that of a mediaeval slipper.

Lotus is one of the commonest members of the pea family in the Peak District, not least because it tolerates a wide range of soil types. It grows on well-drained, unimproved grassland where it withstands grazing. It is also found on roadsides, on the poor soils of limestone quarry waste and as a metal-tolerant race on the spoil heaps of the old lead mines. The nitrogen-fixing properties of the bacteria contained in its root nodules facilitate its growth on nutrient-poor soils. Agricultural grassland and landscaping schemes such as new road verges are often seeded with *Lotus* but the sown strain is a non-native variant with erect growth (to 60 cm) and much larger leaves than the wild type.

Bird's-foot-trefoil is a mostly hairless perennial (to 20 cm) with a spreading, solid stem and a woody base (see illustration). Despite its name, the leaves consist of 5 leaflets (each up to 1 cm wide), the lowest pair are often thought to be stipules but the true stipules are tiny and brown. The long-stalked flower-heads bear from 2–7 yellow-petalled 'pea' flowers that have red veins on the rear (standard) petal. The flattened buds are tipped a deep orange-red. Flowering continues from May to October. The slender fruit pods twist and split open to release their seeds.

Lotus is a food plant for the caterpillars of an infrequent Peak butterfly, the Green Hairstreak. The photograph shows another insect visitor the Six-spot Burnet. Greater Bird's-foot-trefoil (*Lotus pedunculatus*) occurs in damper habitats. It is an erect, taller plant (to 50 cm) with hollow stems, broader leaflets and more crowded flower-heads of larger flowers. Common Bird's-foot-trefoil is a very variable plant in relation to leaf shape, size and hairiness and also petal colour—in some plants the open flower retains the orange-red of the bud. The garden cultivar 'Plenus' which is grown in rockeries, is a smaller plant with double flowers.

Illustration by Sue James

Pea Family *Fabaceae or Leguminosae*

Kidney Vetch Anthyllis vulneraria

Former common names such as Lamb-toe and Granny's Pincushion as well as the Latin *Anthyllis* all reflect the appearance of the mass of soft grey sepals in the flower-head. Locally it was called Lady's Fingers, a name also given to *Lotus corniculatus* (see page 82) but here it refers to the finger-like leaf bracts below the flower-head and not, as in *Lotus*, to the fruit pods. The Latin *vulneraria* and the common name Staunch, bear witness to its former use as a vulnerary. It is the kidney-shaped flower-head that has provided the most widespread common name. Under the doctrine that plant features were a clue to their potential medicinal use we find Charles Lyte writing in 1578 that it 'prevayle much against the hoate pisse—or difficultie to make water'.

Kidney Vetch is locally frequent on dry limestone grassland and rocky outcrops, especially on dale sides in the White Peak and also on old railway tracks and by roads built with limestone in both the White and Dark Peak. It often grows with plants such as Salad Burnet (*Sanguisorba minor*) and Common Rock-rose (*Helianthemum nummularium* see page 80) and is the food-plant of the Small Blue butterfly.

Anthyllis is a softly hairy perennial with either erect or spreading stems. The lowest leaves are very variable and as the illustration shows some consist of just one, long-petioled blade, the others are compound and up to 6 cm long, with opposite pairs of leaflets and a larger terminal one. Upper leaves are sessile, with narrower, equal-sized leaflets. The leaves are silky-white below. Two flower-heads are compacted together and surrounded by a ruff of green, finger-like bracts (modified leaves). Each small flower (there are about 20 in a group) consists of 5 fused, inflated woolly sepals (often with red-fringed apical teeth) and yellow petals in the shape of a pea flower. The dead brown flowers are retained for some time (see illustration) and are more noticeable than the tiny, jointed seed pods.

There is considerable variation within the species and some authors have attempted to divide the group into a number of subspecies. Flower colour variants are common and include orange and flesh-pink, while the red form, found on Cornish cliffs, is sold by nurseries as var. *coccinea*. The closely packed flowers and the leaf shape help prevent confusion with the commoner Bird's-foot-trefoil (*Lotus corniculatus*). The similar but smaller, Horse-shoe Vetch (*Hippocrepis comosa*) is a rare plant in the Peak District. It has *Lotus*-like flower-heads of small, plain-yellow flowers and leaves with up to 21 small, oblong leaflets. The sinuous pods break up into horseshoe-like sections.

Illustration by Primrose Lawton

Pea Family *Fabaceae or Leguminosae*

Bitter Vetch Lathyrus linifolius var. montanus

With its winged stem and relatively few leaflets this plant is more closely related to the garden Perennial Sweet Pea (*Lathyrus latifolius*) than to other wild vetches. The Latin *montanus* (it was previously known as *Lathyrus montanus*) refers to its distribution, it being predominantly a plant of upland districts in the north and west. Where it occurs in lowland England it is mostly confined to ancient woodland. Old local names include Nipper Nuts and the Yorkshire term Peasling. Gerard refers to 'The Nuts of this Pease being boiled and eaten' but it was not the tiny pea-like seeds that were consumed. Bitter Vetch refers to the sharp taste of the 'nuts' (which are actually swollen tuberous parts of the underground rhizome).

The preferred habitat of Bitter Vetch is moist, neutral or slightly acidic soil. It is local in the Peak and not easy to find after July when flowering has finished. With an erect habit it is susceptible to over-grazing in the early part of the year. It occurs on the brows of the dales (where the calcium content of the soil is not high), on moorland margins and is also associated with volcanic intrusions such as that at Tideswell Dale quarry.

Lathyrus is an erect, hairless perennial growing to 40 cm high. The green, winged stem bears alternate compound leaves that are made up of 2,3 or 4 pairs of blue-green, parallel-veined leaflets. These are either elliptical (as shown in the illustration) or more linear. There is no tendril, the terminal leaflet being reduced to a tiny point. The leaf-like stipules at the leaf base are minutely toothed. The pea-like flowers, which are produced from late April, are borne in heads of 2–6 on the end of long stalks. Initially a deep red they quickly fade to purple and then blue-green, giving the appearance of having been painted with water-colour that has run! The straight, hairless, dark-brown pods (up to 4 cm long) twist and split before releasing the seeds.

Bitter Vetch appears to be decreasing and does not easily spread from seed. Where it occurs it may spread over many metres but this is largely due to vegetative reproduction from the rhizome. Perhaps digging up the plant for food in earlier times did not help, though most records of this are from Scotland where it was dried and eaten like chewing gum and even used to flavour whisky! Naturalised garden escapes of *Lathyrus* species have much wider leaflets and many more larger flowers.

Illustration by Cyril Stocks

Figwort Family *Scrophulariaceae*

Yellow Rattle *Rhinanthus minor*

The generic name for this plant comes from two Greek words meaning 'nose' and 'flower'. It was previously called *Rhinanthus crista-galli*, the specific term coming from the similarity of the flower bract to that of a cockerel's comb. The common names are all connected with the shape of, and noise made by, the fruit. They include Hen-penny, Penny-grass, Money in a Purse, and Hay Rattle. The latter relates to its formerly common habitat of hay meadows. It is an annual and by the time of the hay cut it had already produced its penny-like seeds. The move to cutting grass for silage (with the first cut much earlier in the summer) has eliminated this plant from many of its former sites.

Yellow Rattle is a semi-parasite, its roots taking water and nutrients from surrounding grass and clover plants. It cannot stand grazing or trampling and in the Peak District is mostly confined to old meadows and uncut road verges on limestone, neutral or mildly acidic soils. It is far less common than it was even 30 years ago, but where it does occur it often forms dense patches. It is very variable and some botanists have attempted to create 6 different subspecies, despite the fact that many populations contain a mix of these.

The angled, erect stem grows to about 40 cm and branches regularly from the leaf axils. The smooth, green stems are liberally spotted with purple-brown (see illustration). The rather blue-green, narrow sessile leaves have toothed margins and are produced in opposite pairs with each pair at 90 degrees to its neighbours.

Flowers appear from mid summer onwards. Each flower (on little or no stalk) arises from the axil of a bract (like a broad leaf). The pale green sepals are fused into a flattened globe for most of their length but end in 4 pointed teeth. The sepals are suffused with purple on the veins and are minutely hairy on the teeth margins. Most of the petal tube is hidden by the sepals, but two lips are exposed: the upper one is laterally compressed and curves down towards the three-lobed lower one. The petals are either a uniform yellow or include shades of brown, with a violet tooth either side of the upper lip. The single, penny-shaped, winged seed develops within the, still inflated, sepal tube.

In addition to the change to silage, former habitats for Yellow Rattle in the Peak District have been ploughed and re-sown or have had fertilisers applied. All of these actions have reduced the frequency of this once-common plant.

Illustration by Judy Pickles

Orchid family *Orchidaceae*

Common Spotted Orchid *Dactylorhiza fuchsii*

The generic name for this orchid can be loosely translated as 'finger-like root' a theme that is repeated in common names such as Dead Men's Fingers. In Hamlet, Shakespeare writes of 'Long Purples' which some scholars have taken to mean Early-purple Orchid but, in a later reference, he uses the name Dead Men's Fingers. This confusion between the two orchid species is still found today and is compounded by both having spotted leaves. The specific *fuchsii* honours the 16th-century German botanist, Leonard Fuchs who included a drawing of the plant in his History of Plants published in 1542. (The genus *Fuchsia* is also named after him.)

This orchid is a plant of lime-rich soils and is locally abundant in places in the White Peak, especially in open woodland and on grassy dale sides. It has successfully colonised the spoil heaps of disused limestone quarries and lead workings as well as old railway cuttings. Where it occurs on the millstone grit it is usually associated with the importation of limestone, such as for road building. The related Heath Spotted Orchid (*Dactylorhiza maculata*) grows on acid, peaty soils but is surprisingly infrequent in the Peak District, even on the moorlands.

Common Spotted Orchid has hand-like, underground tubers. The lower, dull-green, fleshy leaves are broadly elliptical (up to 4 cm wide) the upper much narrower and more grass-like. The leaves are keeled and densely spotted with transverse purple blotches (in contrast to those in Early-purple Orchid which are elongated along the leaf) but some plants have unspotted leaves. The head (to 50 cm) of pale-pink (occasionally white) flowers is borne on a solid stem from June to late July. The spreading, lateral, petal-like sepals and the front lip are liberally marked with red-purple lines (in contrast to Early-purple Orchid). The middle of three lobes on the lip is typically the longest. The back of the flower ends in a straight, down-pointing spur.

The genus *Dactylorhiza* includes the Marsh Orchids that have hollow stems and these form hybrids with the Spotted Orchids in a few sites in the Peak. The resulting plants are often much larger and the flower-spikes are considerably longer. Heath Spotted Orchid has narrower leaves (with more circular spots) and flowers in which the middle lobe of the front lip is smaller than the others.

Illustration by Cyril Stocks

Orchid family *Orchidaceae*

Fly Orchid *Ophrys insectifera*

The Fly Orchid is a less flamboyant relative of the Bee Orchid (see page 104). An older Latin name was *Ophrys muscifera* from *Musca*, the insect genus that includes the House-fly. In fact the flower bears more resemblance to a Bluebottle. Fly Orchid is a rare plant in Britain and there are only 7 current sites in the whole of Derbyshire.

In the Peak District it is a plant of limestone soils and occurs in grassland (especially where there is shade from bushes or spaced trees), open woodland and, like many other orchids, on the floor and spoil heaps of disused quarry workings. Some of the Peak populations are within Sites of Special Scientific Interest where they have some legal protection, but other sites are vulnerable to changes in agricultural practice and new quarrying activity. Even in known sites it is not an easy orchid to detect.

Fly Orchid, like the other members of the genus *Ophrys*, has two swollen, undivided underground tubers. The rather few, unspotted, bright-green leaves are broadly elliptical and mostly near the base of the long (to 60 cm), slender stem. The flowers, which are longer than they are wide, are very widely spaced on the stem and there are often fewer than six flowers on any one plant. The flowers open in June, usually about two weeks earlier than those of Bee Orchid.

Each flower has three narrow, spreading, yellow-green sepals. Of the petals, two are thread-like, purple-brown and velvety. They are held erect, rather like the antennae of an insect (see illustration). The third, a lip petal (labellum) has two lateral, hairy lobes and one elongated, dark red-brown middle lobe that is divided at its apex into two, blunt-ended sections. The lip is held flat, unlike the deeply convex shape of the comparable part in the Bee Orchid. In the centre of this lip, just below the two side lobes, there is a shiny, slate-blue patch with a sheen similar to that seen on the bodies of Bluebottles and some wasp species.

The orange-red anther forms a hood at the top end of the labellum and this bears a pair of pollinia (pollen masses). The flowers are regularly cross-pollinated by male solitary wasps in the genus *Agogorytes* which land on the lip and attempt copulation (having presumably mistaken the flower for a female). During this process the pollinia become stuck to the wasp—being transferred to another plant when the insect is once again fooled by the mimicry of the flowers.

Illustration by Cyril Stocks

Geranium Family *Geraniaceae*

Meadow Cranesbill *Geranium pratense*

Geranium comes from the Greek word geranos meaning a crane, a bird with a long tapering bill. The Geranium fruit is shaped like a crane's bill, hence the name. Confusion is created by the fact that many people also use the name Geranium for the many cultivars of *Pelargonium* grown in greenhouses and used as bedding plants. These are not native and differ from *Geranium* species in their clustered flower heads and less spectacular fruits.

Geranium pratense is uncommon as a wild plant in southern England but is locally abundant in damp meadows, by streams and on some roadside verges in the Peak District. It mostly occurs on the limestone, typically on the moister north and west-facing dale sides where it often grows with other tall herbs such as Marjoram (see page 128) and Angelica. It also occurs as a road-verge plant in the Dark Peak, probably as a result of the use of limestone in the road construction. Its deep blue flowers are produced through the summer months, one apt local name for the plant is Thunderclouds.

Meadow Cranesbill is a tall (to a metre), clump-forming perennial and, in contrast to Bloody Cranesbill (see page 96), has many dark green leaves with long petioles arising from the plant base.(Illustration shows dying basal leaf at bottom right). The large blade (up to 12 cm across) is deeply cut into 5–7 lobes, each of which is further divided, with toothed margins. Both sides are slightly downy. The smaller stem leaves have little or no stalk and narrower lobes. The main stem and flower stalks are hairy and in the upper parts of the plant these hairs are sticky and glandular.

The flowers are usually borne in pairs on slightly drooping stalks, the drooping being more pronounced after rain. Each blue-violet petal is beautifully veined and is rounded at its apex. As the illustration shows, the young fruits hang down but as they mature they become erect and finally split open with the five one-seeded sections springing apart from the base.

Meadow Cranesbill is an easily cultivated plant of herbaceous borders from where it may escape into the wild. In late summer, the leaves exhibit orange, purple and red-brown hues—especially on plants growing in open situations. There are a large number of cultivars including double-flowered forms (with a long flowering season) and others in which flower colour ranges from white to deep violet.

Illustration by Sylvia Ford

Geranium Family *Geraniaceae*

Bloody Cranesbill *Geranium sanguineum*

The Victorians were not happy with the common name of this plant and tried to change it to the Blood Red Cranesbill but the swearers won the day! The Latin term *sanguineum* also refers to blood, a common misconception is that the plant was named after the blood-red colour of its flowers but, as the illustration shows, the flowers are not blood-red. The stems, however, are, especially at the swollen branches, and it is this feature that gave rise to the name.

Bloody Cranesbill is one of the most striking native plants of the White Peak, where the large flowers seem to glow in the sunshine. It is locally frequent around limestone outcrops and in older scree slopes on exposed dale sides or under open scrub or woodland. Every year thousands of visitors to Miller's Dale enjoy seeing this beautiful plant growing by the roadside and in the old railway cuttings.

It is a perennial and forms well-branched clumps to 40 cm high. The stems are usually erect but in exposed habitats may trail on the ground. They are sparsely covered with long spreading hairs and the orange-red colour is deepest at the knee-like joints where they branch. Plants from more shaded habitats show less red on the stem. The dark green leaves are up to 6 cm across (the largest being the few which arise from the base of the plant on long petioles) with 5–7 deeply cut lobes, most of which are further subdivided into three segments. Both sides are covered with appressed hairs. The large flowers (up to 4 cm across) are produced from June to August. Each is at the end of a long, erect stalk that also bears a pair of tiny reduced leaves. The 5 petals can best be described as magenta, or crimson-purple, and are shallowly notched at their tip. As with the other Cranesbills occasional white-flowered plants occur. The typical long-beaked fruit is shown at the centre of the illustration.

A look through a range of books with colour pictures of Bloody Cranesbill will show what appears to be a difference of opinion as to the true colour of the flower, however, observations recorded over 400 years ago help to explain this situation. Each flower stays open for some three or four days. On the first day of opening it is a rich magenta-red but by the second day it has deepened to mulberry and on the third day there is a distinct purple-blue tint to the flower. One thing is certain, they are not the colour of blood!

Geranium sanguineum is a popular rock garden plant and a number of cultivars are available including one with white flowers and, 'Striatum', with flesh-pink flowers.

Illustration by Margaret Wightman

Phlox Family *Polemoniaceae*

Jacob's Ladder *Polemonium caeruleum*

The Book of Genesis (chapter 28 verse 12) tells of the dream of Jacob who saw a ladder reaching to heaven. This plant is topped with sky-blue (heavenly?) flowers and has leaves with many leaflets, like the rungs of a ladder. It has long been grown in gardens where it is also known as Greek Valerian. Culpeper mentioned its medicinal uses as being similar to that of Valerian (*Valeriana officinalis*, see page 116) and others report that, as with Valerian, cats are fond of rolling in *Polemonium*. Despite its popularity as a garden plant (from where it may become naturalised) it is very rare as a native British species.

In the Peak District it is locally frequent in a small number of sites, usually in long grassland, on scree slopes and on rocky ledges in the limestone dales. It is usually found on shady, north-facing slopes where it is often associated with species such as Meadowsweet *(Filipendula vulgaris)*, Dog's Mercury *(Mercurialis perennis)*, and Valerian. The populations, such as that in Lathkill Dale, are very long established but pollen records show that before the final retreat of the last ice-age the plant was much more frequent across England. Why it retreated to so few localities and does not readily recolonise former sites is still a mystery but is probably associated with changing climatic conditions and factors such as altered grazing pressure which prevent the successful establishment of its seedlings.

Jacob's Ladder is a perennial, with a short rhizome and erect hollow stems bearing many compound leaves. It grows to 1 metre tall when in flower. The long-petioled, basal leaves (up to 35 cm long) consist of up to 12 pairs of pointed leaflets, the final pair being fused at their bases with the single terminal leaflet (see illustration). Smaller leaves with fewer leaflets and little or no petiole are found higher up the stem. The drooping flowers, which appear in June and July and are up to 3 cm across, have 5 blue (rarely white) petals. These form a tight, central, throat from which the stamens emerge on long purple-blue filaments. Unusually for a Dicotyledon, the style is three-lobed (see illustration). The erect fruit capsules are formed within the persistent sepals.

In gardens, where it does best in partial shade, it readily grows from seed and often behaves as a biennial, frequently having paler coloured flowers than the wild type. A number of American species of *Polemonium* are also cultivated.

Illustration by Juliet Regan

Plantain Family *Plantaginaceae*

Hoary Plantain *Plantago media*

Of the several different species of Plantain found growing in the Peak District, this is undoubtedly the most beautiful and, on more than one occasion, students of botany have mistaken it for a wild orchid. Its highly scented, pink flower-head (an old name was Scent Bottle) is a far cry from the green-brown flowers of the rest of the genus. The Latin planta means 'the sole of the foot' and both Greater Plantain (*Plantago major*) and Hoary Plantain have broadly ovate leaf blades reminiscent of the shape of a sole. The leaves of both species are produced in a basal rosette and are held flat to the ground thus making them tolerant of being trodden on—another link with soles!

Plantago media is a plant of neutral and calcium-rich soils and is far more frequent in the White Peak where it forms part of the short (grazed) turf grassland on the dales, it is also found in old pastures and hay meadows. It has an interesting association with churchyards (one wonders if there is a link with a high calcium level from the bones?) which I learnt as a young botanist when I found it in a Bracknell churchyard as the only record for that part of Berkshire.

The leaves that form the basal rosette have a broadly oval or diamond-shaped blade which is grey-green in colour and covered with downy hairs, especially on the 5–9 prominent, parallel veins. The blade margin has a few small teeth and unlike the smoother Greater Plantain, the blade gradually narrows to the petiole that is much shorter than the blade. The flower spike, which is up to 6 cm, is at the end of a long (to 30 cm) unfurrowed, leafless stalk (scape). The tiny, scented flowers appear from May to August and those at the base of the spike open first. The petals are white and inconspicuous but the pink stamens, borne on purple stalks, provide a haze of colour. The plant is pollinated by insects, unlike the other Plantains which are wind pollinated.

The leaves contain tannin and have long been used medicinally for their astringent properties. Shakespeare, in Romeo and Juliet explained that Plantain leaf was excellent for a broken shin. The seeds are rich in mucilage and these were boiled in milk to provide a mild laxative. The related Greater Plantain was one of the sacred herbs of the Anglo-Saxons because of its medical properties. A Rose-flowered form of Hoary Plantain (a mutation which results in a much wider flower-head) seems to have been lost from cultivation. The most popular garden species is *Plantago nivalis* which is grown for its hairy, silver-green, lance-shaped leaves.

Illustration by Anne Dent

Orchid Family *Orchidaceae*

Fragrant Orchid *Gymnadenia conopsea*

Unlike the unpleasant smell of the Early-purple Orchid (see page 62) this graceful species has a more acceptable fragrance, hence its common name. Smell however is one of the more subjective of the senses and its scent has been compared with vanilla, clove and Mock Orange (*Philadelphus*), odours that not everyone finds agreeable. Early morning sniffers are more likely to ask 'what fragrance?' as the scent is at its strongest in the evening.

Fragrant Orchid is far less common than either Early-purple or Common Spotted Orchid in the Peak District and is restricted to the limestone regions. It is locally frequent in parts of Miller's Dale, at Longstone Edge and Via Gellia. It grows in short grassland and most of its sites are on disturbed ground such as that resulting from quarrying (where it is found on the floor of disused quarries and on the spoil banks) or the laying of railway tracks.

Gymnadenia has several underground tubers, which divide to form long, tapering, finger-like projections. Most of the leaves are unspotted (in contrast to those of Early Purple and Common Spotted Orchid) glossy, deeply keeled and ranked on opposite sides of the stem. The lower leaves are hooded at the tip unlike the smaller upper leaves, which hug the stem. The long flower spike (to 40 cm) is cylindrical when all the flowers are open but it is more conical in the bud stage (see illustration) when it can be confused with that of Pyramidal Orchid—though this has a shorter, denser flower-head (see page 112). Each flower emerges from the axil of a green, leaf-like bract. The lilac-pink flowers are unspotted and the front lip is three-lobed at its apex. The most noticeable feature is the very long, pointed spur (to 2 cm long) which projects down from the back of the flower before curling outwards (see illustration). In the bud stage the spurs from neighbouring flowers overlap like crossed swords.

Some taxonomists have divided the species into several subspecies. The one shown is subspecies *conopsea*, which is typically found on well-drained soils. In the Peak District, Fragrant Orchid comes into flower slightly later than the Spotted Orchid and at about the same time as Bee Orchid, that is from late June and through July.

Illustration by Sheila Stancil

Orchid Family *Orchidaceae*

Bee Orchid *Ophrys apifera*

For many people this is perhaps the most exotic looking of all our native plants and it is probably among the most photographed. *Ophrys* comes from the Greek for 'eyebrow' and in Pliny's time, women used an extract of the plant to darken their eyebrows. Fortunately, for the plant, there are now easier alternatives for this practice! The specific name *apifera* means 'bee bearing', *Apis* being the insect genus that includes the Honey Bee. The flowers actually resemble not a Honey Bee but a Bumble, or Humble Bee, so a more apt specific name would be *bombifera*. In the 16th century Gerard called it the Humble-bee Flower and in the West Country it was long known as Bumble Bee.

Bee Orchid is not as rare in the Peak District as Pyramidal Orchid (see page 112) but it is very local in occurrence. Numbers fluctuate and the proportion of plants bearing flowers can vary greatly from one year to the next. Most, if not all, of the sites are man-made or in areas that have been disturbed, and include several nature reserves in disused quarries (e.g. Miller's Dale and Hopton).

As the illustration shows, Bee Orchid has 2 swollen tubers, which are undivided. The rather grey-green leaves, which form a basal rosette are oval in shape and without spots. The stem (which can reach over 40 cm) bears narrower leaves, which get smaller and more bract-like towards the top of the plant. Each stem typically bears only about 5 flowers, each arising from the axil of a green bract, from late June and through July. Flowers are up to 3 cm across and lack of number is more than compensated for by their colour and form. The 3, spreading, pointed sepals are pink with green veins and are much larger than the 2 blunt-ended upper petals. The third petal forms the lip (labellum) that resembles the body of a Bumble Bee. The 2 lateral lobes are hairy and a paler colour. The central lobe is deeply convex and ends in a tiny tooth that is curled up behind (and often out of sight). The deep brown colour is marked with yellow-orange markings, the exact pattern of which is different in each individual.

In newly opened flowers, 2 long-stalked yellow pollinia (pollen masses) hang from the green anther which looks like a duck's head (see inset photo with just one pollinium remaining). It was previously thought that these were carried from one plant to another by male bees in the act of pseudocopulation (see page 92 Fly Orchid) but it appears that in Britain at least, most of the flowers are self-pollinated.

Illustration by Dorothy Bramley

Heath Family *Ericaceae*

Cross-leaved Heath *Erica tetralix*

Erica comes from the Greek ereiko meaning 'a heath'. The specific *tetralix* refers to the whorls of leaves in fours, the cross-like nature of the leaves generating the common name. Before Linnaeus popularised the binomial system of Latin names this plant was known as *Erica pumila calyculato unedonis flore* meaning 'the little heath with the small calyx and a flower like a strawberry-tree!' A common name still in use is Maiden's Blush—an apt, if sexist, description of its flower colour. Female associations are also found in the old name She-heather (in contrast to the coarser He-heather or Ling, see page 136). It was also known as Bog-heather, a reference to its wet moorland habitat.

Cross-leaved Heath is far less common than Heather in the Peak District and is largely restricted to waterlogged acid moorland in the Dark Peak. It is usually associated with wet areas and Sphagnum moss. Knowledgeable walkers avoid treading on it for fear of getting wet feet! It often occurs as just a small number of plants, in contrast to the huge tracts of Heather.

Erica tetralix is a small evergreen shrub, typically up to 30 cm. The lower part of the stem is woody and branched but all the branches end in a group of flowers and there are no short side branches as in Heather. Young stems are downy. Each rather grey-green, scarcely stalked leaf (produced in whorls of four) is covered with sticky hairs and appears to have a pale midrib on the undersurface. Closer inspection shows that the leaf blade is rolled under from the margins, the central white stripe being the gap between the leaf edges. As the illustration shows, the leaves below the flower heads are less crowded and tend to hug the stem. Flowering starts in July (much earlier than Heather) and each compact, terminal cluster bears up to 12 flowers. 4 small, deeply lobed, sticky sepals surround the base of the 4 much larger, rose-pink (occasionally white) petals that are fused to form a globe with a constricted opening. The drooping buds and flowers gradually become erect as the flower head ages.

This is one of the most attractive of our Heaths but (possibly because of its water requirement) there are fewer cultivars than there are of our other native Heaths. A favourite one is 'Alba Mollis' which has silvery-grey leaves and pure white flowers. Many of our garden Ericas are cultivars of the closely related Irish Heath (*Erica mackaiana*) which has similar flower clusters but less-hairy, only slightly inrolled leaves.

Illustration by Mary Acton

Heath Family *Ericaceae*

Bell Heather *Erica cinerea*

This species gets its common name from the shape of its flowers, which are also highlighted in the local name Bell Ling. It was previously also known as Carlin Heather and Crow Ling. It is occasionally called Fine-leaved Heath and its leaves are indeed the slenderest of the three species found in the Peak District.

Bell Heather requires well drained, acid soil so is rarely found beside the wet-loving *Erica tetralix* (see page 106) but often grows with Bilberry (*Vaccinium myrtillus*) and Cowberry (*Vaccinium vitis-idaea*). It is more susceptible to grazing than other Heathers and is locally frequent on steep clough slopes below the higher moors as it is also more frost sensitive. It also grows on roadsides, gritstone outcrops and on old quarry ledges of the Dark Peak—all sites which are relatively dry and less accessible to grazing sheep. It is most frequent on south-facing slopes and starts flowering from mid-June and is the earliest of the three Peak District Heathers to flower.

Erica cinerea is a small, evergreen shrub with older grey-brown stems (*cinerea* means ashy-grey) from which flowering branches grow to a height of about 50 cm. Only the young shoots are hairy. The dark green leaves are very tightly down-rolled and, in contrast to Cross-leaved Heath, are almost hairless and borne in threes. Masses of further leaves are produced on very short branches in the axils of these main leaves.

Flowers are formed near the ends of the stems but, unlike Cross-leaved Heath, are only rarely restricted to a group at the apex. Each flower consists of 4 small, pointed, purple sepals at the base of the 4, much larger, petals which are fused in the shape of a bell but with a restricted opening. Petal colour varies from a rich crimson-purple to a deep rose-pink. White-flowered individuals are less common than they are with Ling.

The tightly down-rolled leaves of Bell Heather significantly reduce the amount of water loss through the breathing pores (stomata). This enables the plant to grow on south-facing, dry, rocky slopes where other species might suffer from lack of water. This species is equally at home in a dry garden and there are many cultivars, some have white flowers, others a more beetroot-red colour, most having been collected from the wild. Many cultivars are grown for their bronzed or golden foliage.

Illustration by Primrose Lawton

Rose Family *Rosaceae*

Cloudberry *Rubus chamaemorus*

Cloudberry is a mountain plant and though Gerard (1597) indicated that it grew 'where clouds are lower than the tops [of the mountain] all winter long' and that this was the origin of the name, it is more likely that (as Grigson states) the name actually comes from the Old English 'clud' berry or berry on a rocky hill. Locally it was also known as Knotberry and a knot also meant a hill. As with a number of other plants depicted in this book, Cloudberry is near the southern edge of its British range in the Peak District.

Rubus chamaemorus is restricted to the Dark Peak where it grows on the drier, more eroded areas of the very acid, blanket peat, typically at an altitude of at least 1,500 feet (c. 460 metres). In Victorian times it was far more common than it is today, and the fruit was collected for sale. Even 30 years ago it was described as locally frequent on the northern moorlands but today it is less common (though the head of the Derwent Valley is still a stronghold) and flowers and fruits are rarely seen. This is partly because it is a shy flowerer but also because many of the nutrient-rich flowers are eaten by sheep. Any fruit which forms is also likely to be eaten by sheep, or grouse, leaving very little for human consumption!

Cloudberry is a relative of Raspberry (*Rubus idaeus*) but is low growing, with the non-spiny, flowering stems rarely exceeding 20 cm. Rather few, large, 5–7 palmately lobed, bright-green leaves emerge from an underground rhizome in late spring. The leaves are slightly hairy (especially on the petioles) and have a toothed margin. Cloudberry has separate sex plants and the male plants have more deeply lobed leaves.

The solitary flowers (2–3 cm across) appear from June through into August and bear 5, pointed green sepals and 5 (rarely 4) white petals. Flowers on male plants bear a mass of yellow stamens (see illustration) while those on female plants (which appear to be less frequent and this is another reason for a shortage of fruit) contain the stigmas. The fruit is like that of a Blackberry but with far fewer, larger segments. Initially green it turns red before finally ripening a rich orange colour.

The increasing number of accidental summer fires coupled with a much higher grazing pressure from sheep in recent years is thought to have been instrumental in the decline of Cloudberry in the Peak District.

Illustration by Cate Wildman

Orchid Family *Orchidaceae*

Pyramidal Orchid *Anacamptis pyramidalis*

This beautiful orchid gets its name from the pyramid shape of the dense flower spike but, when all the flowers are out, the flower head is much more cylindrical. The flowers are very compacted into a short spike (no more than 5 cm), in contrast to the much longer spike found in Fragrant Orchid, which sometimes grows in the same sites as *Anacamptis* and may be confused with it.

Pyramidal Orchid is, sadly, not common in the Peak District. A recent report shows that for the whole of Derbyshire there are only 10 sites where it has been recorded since 1980. It is a plant of short limestone grassland, many of its sites are on disturbed ground including those in or close to limestone quarries or lead spoil heaps being worked for fluorite. Fortunately some colonies are in Sites of Special Scientific Interest, others are in Nature Reserves but the possibility of new workings, together with a lack of grazing (which removes competitors) threatens the long term survival of this species at some of its current sites.

Anacamptis has two ovoid root tubers. The lower, pale grey-green leaves are broadly lanceolate (with a sharp-pointed apex) and form a rosette at the stem base. Each upper leaf is smaller and the lower part sheaths the flower stem. Pyramidal Orchid rarely flowers in the Peak District before the end of June and in poor summers flowers can be seen as late as early August. The individual flowers are typically a deep pink but there is considerable variation in colour even within a colony, some individuals are white flowered, others more red-purple. Unlike a number of other pink-flowered Orchids, the flowers of Pyramidal Orchid are without spots or lines of different colours. Each flower has three upper tepals and two laterals above the front lip. This latter part is deeply divided into three lobes and bears two raised plates in its central region. The spur, which is very slender and about the same length as the green ovary beneath the petals, projects down from the back of the flower.

Each flower is borne on a twisted stalk. Occasional mutant forms of Pyramidal Orchid may be found which lack this twist and thus have all the flowers 'upside down'. It looks very odd but is not a new species! The flowers are pollinated by moths, including the black and red Six-spot Burnet moth which is a day flying species (see page 82).

Illustration by Dorothy Bramley

Orchid Family *Orchidaceae*

Frog Orchid *Coeloglossum viride*

This is one of our smaller and less showy orchids in which the flower is described in the Latin name as a 'hollow green tongue'. Green, however is not the only colour as the flowers are a mix of olive-green, yellow-green and red-brown, a similar colour mix to that found in the Common Frog. It is infrequent in the Peak District but its small size and subtle colours mean that it is easily overlooked and is possibly under-recorded.

As with many of the other Orchid species of the Peak District, Frog Orchid is a plant of limestone grassland in the White Peak and is most frequently recorded growing in disturbed habitats. It occurs on spoil mounds of disused quarries and on mounds of overburden created during the installation of the railways. A good example of this latter habitat is to be found near the old signal box at Hartington where a mound supports a large colony of Frog Orchids. Frog Orchid even grows on spoil heaps associated with the lead rakes as well as on old pastures and other less disturbed limestone habitats.

Frog Orchid is a perennial with a number of palmately branched root tubers. The plant can attain a height of 25 cm but even when in full flower it is frequently less than 10 cm. At the stem base are two or three broad oval leaves with a blunt apex (the lowest leaf may be almost circular in outline). The hairless leaves are unspotted and have parallel veins. The few upper leaves are much smaller and narrower. The short stem is often a yellow-brown in its upper region (see illustration) and slightly ribbed.

The short spike of lightly honey-scented flowers opens from June onwards, each flower forming in the axil of a narrow green bract. The three sepals and two upper petals curve over to form a 'helmet' at the top of the flower. This is usually an olive-green colour with red-brown edges. The other petal forms the lip, or labellum, which hangs vertically below the 'helmet'. The parallel-sided, tongue-like lip is three-lobed at its apex, the middle lobe being the shortest. It too is green with red-brown margins (see illustration).

Illustration by Sheila Stancil

Valerian family *Valerianaceae*

Valerian *Valeriana officinalis*

This native species is frequently confused with Red (or Wall) Valerian (*Centranthus ruber*) which was introduced to our gardens in the 16th century and is frequently grown as a cottage garden plant in the Peak District. Red Valerian has rather fleshy, simple, grey-green leaves and dark pink or white flowers—in contrast to the true Valerian that has green, compound leaves and very pale-pink flower-heads. Valeria was a Roman province, Valerius an early herbalist and valere comes from the Latin meaning 'to be well'. The specific name *officinalis* indicates that it was a plant sold for medicinal use. Its medicinal virtues are noted in the name All-heal, while the old Yorkshire name Cat-trail relates to its former use by cat catchers—its smell causing great excitement to cats. Some authorities hint that it was also used by rat catchers and suspect that Valerian root in the Pied Piper's pocket was the rat lure rather than his music!

Valerian is a very variable plant, it is frequent in rough pasture and disturbed sites (quarries, railway tracks etc.) in the White Peak and also in wet habitats such as by rivers and streams in both the White and Dark Peak. It thrives on cliff ledges and other sites out of reach of sheep as its succulent leaves are susceptible to grazing. Some authorities consider that there are two different subspecies each with different habitat requirements but more research is needed to confirm this.

It is a perennial with erect, grooved, hollow stems (glabrous except at the base) which reach 150 cm and may produce short stolons. The dark-green, hairless, compound leaves are borne in pairs, each consisting of up to 9 pairs (plus one terminal) of lanceolate, toothed (rarely entire) leaflets. Basal leaves have a long petiole but upper stem leaves are sessile and much shorter. Flowering is from June to August, the tiny flowers, with pinkish-white petals and smelling strongly of vanilla, are massed in terminal, umbel-like heads some 5–10 cm across.

The dried rhizome (and roots) smell of sweaty feet and one of the chemical oils extracted from them is also found in human sweat! A tincture of Valerian has long been used as a herbal tranquilliser, to reduce nerve pain, cure insomnia and alleviate nervous tension. Until the 1940s Valerian was cultivated by the 'Valerie growers' of Derbyshire, centred on Chesterfield. Offshoots and seedlings were collected from the Dales and cultivated in well-manured land. Flower-heads were removed to promote bigger rhizome growth. Valium and a host of similar so-called 'safe' synthetic tranquillisers have largely replaced the use of Valerian.

Illustration by Amanda Willoughby

Figwort Family *Scrophulariaceae*

Monkey Flower *Mimulus guttatus*

Linnaeus named the genus to which this species belongs after the word 'mimus' meaning an actor. The flowers are face-like in appearance and this particular species is said to be reminiscent of the face of a grinning monkey. The specific name *guttatus* means 'spotted' and though this is a feature of the flower, a closely related species, Blood-drop Emlets (*Mimulus luteus*), which was introduced from South America, has a more obviously spotted flower. Some garden centres still sell the two species wrongly labelled. In 1826 the plant hunter David Douglas introduced Musk (*Mimulus moschatus*) and this smaller-flowered, strongly scented plant became a garden favourite until it mysteriously lost its scent just after the Great War.

Monkey Flower was first observed growing in the wild, in Wales in 1824, following its introduction as a garden plant from the Aleutian islands off Alaska just 12 years previously. It is a plant of wet places and has since spread across most of Britain along rivers, streams and the canal system. In the Peak District it is locally frequent on rocks at the edge of the Rivers Derwent, Wye and Dove. It also occurs in the Cromford Canal, in stream beds and old mill ponds. In places it grows with plants such as Butterbur (*Petasites hybridus*) (see page 20) and Water Forget-me-not (*Myosotis scorpiodes*) and gives the impression of being a native species. *Mimulus luteus* has also escaped but it is now thought that most Peak District records of this are actually of the sterile hybrid between *guttatus* and *luteus*.

Mimulus guttatus is a stoloniferous perennial with a weak, hollow stem that is hairless and often purple-tinged in the lower regions but green and with fine glandular hairs above. The shiny leaves are borne in opposite pairs but only the lower ones are stalked. The margins bear irregular, coarse teeth. The large (to 4 cm) showy flowers arise from the leaf axils on downy stalks. The 5 hairy green sepals are united into a tube for most of their length. The fused, bright-yellow corolla terminates in an upper, two-lobed and a lower, three-lobed lip. The constricted throat of the flower is hairy and dotted with small red spots. After the petals fall, the long protruding style is clearly visible above the sepals which enclose the developing fruit. *Mimulus luteus* has petals with a more open throat (lacking the hairs), with spots and large, red-brown blotches that extend onto the upper and lower lobes.

Monkey Flower is one of the 38 Bach Flower Remedies and it is used to help people to allay fears of events such as going to the dentist. *Mimulus* species are still popular garden plants where they are grown in bog gardens and ponds. Many cultivars exhibit a mix of flower colours and have arisen from hybrids that were first found in the wild.

Illustration by Sylvia Ford

Figwort Family *Scrophulariaceae*

Foxglove *Digitalis purpurea*

Foxglove is a well-known wild plant that has long been grown in gardens and, as such, it is not surprising that it has many common names. These include Bloody Fingers, Fairies Petticoats, Deadmen's Bells, and Poppy; the latter arising from the noise made when unopened flowers are squeezed! The flowers certainly make good finger covers but quite why these should be worn by foxes is less clear. Some authors consider it was a corruption of Folk's Glove, with folk meaning fairies but the original Anglo-Saxon name was 'foxes glova'. The disturbed ground of a fox's den is often colonised by Foxglove seedlings and this link may have been behind the name. The genus name, *Digitalis*, was first coined by Fuchs in 1542 and came from the German for finger, while *purpurea* describes the flower colour.

Digitalis purpurea is a common plant of acid soils and is, therefore, largely absent from limestone regions of the Peak. It is a biennial and the seeds need disturbed ground for successful germination and seedling establishment. As such it is found in hedges (or more typically by walls in the Peak), at the edge of woodland rides and in woods where the soil has been disturbed. It also grows on roadsides and river-banks especially on south-facing sites. Young plants form a basal rosette of leaves that stays green over winter, prior to the production of the flower spike the following summer.

The large ovate, wrinkled leaf blade (to 25 cm long) has a toothed margin and narrows to a winged petiole (see illustration). The upper surface is dark green, the lower more grey-green and downy when young. The terminal portion of the tall (to 2 metres) erect, unbranched stem, forms a one-sided spike of 20–80 nodding flowers. Each separate flower stalk arises from the axil of a small narrow, leaf-like bract. Of the 5 short, green sepals one is typically narrower than the others. The petals are fused into a long tube with 5 small lobes at its apex. The visible upper side is uniformly purple-pink, the lower outer surface is much paler with darker markings, but the inner surface at the mouth of the flower is covered with white spots with red-purple centres and some long hairs. Foxglove is very variable and some plants are much hairier, others have purple stems and there is also a white-flowered form.

Dr William Withering introduced this poisonous plant to orthodox medicine in 1785 (there is a carved foxglove on his memorial) and its constituent chemicals are still used to regulate heartbeat. Many garden cultivars and hybrids produce more horizontally held flowers (ranging from white, through yellow to pink and purple). In contrast to the wild form the flowers are produced from all sides of a much stouter stem.

Illustration by Amanda Willoughby

Iris Family *Iridaceae*

Yellow Iris *Iris pseudacorus*

The *Iris* genus contains species with a wide assortment of flower colours and was named after the Greek word for a rainbow. This, our most common wild species, has a leaf that can be confused with the biblical *Acorus calamus* (Sweet Flag) and the Iris's specific name means 'false Acorus'. It is also known as Yellow Flag on account of the way in which the outer petals flutter in the wind. Some authorities believe that the strange flower shape was the model for the heraldic design of the fleur-de-lys, adopted by Louis VII.

Yellow Iris is a plant of wet pastures and ditches but is most common growing in the shallow water at the margins of rivers, ponds and canals. In the Peak District it is more frequent in some of the river valleys and along the Cromford Canal but is not common on the dry limestone dales or on poor moorland soils. The fluctuating levels of the Peak's reservoirs make them a less suitable habitat than might have been expected. The thick leaves contain air passages that provide a ventilation system down to the rhizome that is frequently waterlogged.

The sword-shaped leaves are held vertically. They have two identical faces that are hairless and a dull blue-green colour. There is a much thickened midrib and occasionally sections to one or both sides of this are wrinkled (see illustration). The leaves consist of blade only, with the lower part sheathing and overlapping the base of other leaves. Basal leaves are up to 3 cm wide and may exceed a metre in length. The showy yellow flowers appear in mid summer. The solid, branched flower stem is oval in cross-section and bears clusters of two or three flowers from within each spathe (a short, cowl-shaped leaf). The large flowers (up to 10 cm across) have a complicated structure. The 3 outer tepals or 'falls' are narrow at the base but then widen and curve downwards. They are beautifully marked with purple veins. The 3 inner 'standards' are shorter, narrower, paler and more erect. Each of the 3 stamens is covered by a yellow, petal-like branch of the style (see central flower in illustration). The large green fruit capsules turn brown before splitting into three to reveal the many seeds.

The plant had a reputation for being apotropaic; that is it averts evil! The rhizome is used in herbal and homoeopathic medicine. Garden cultivars include 'Variegata', with longitudinal white stripes on its leaves. Many other species and hybrids are grown in drier parts of gardens. Sweet Flag is a rare introduction to some of the Peak District canals and differs in its much more wrinkled leaves which smell of tangerines when bruised and also in the finger-like, green flower-head which sticks out like a barber's pole.

Illustration by Juliet Regan

Pea Family *Fabaceae or Leguminosae*

Dyer's Greenweed Genista tinctoria

This plant is like a small version of Broom, *Genista* comes from a Celtic word, gen, meaning 'small bush'. The Latin, tinctorius, means 'as used in dying' as the plant was used to dye cloth yellow, after which the blue dye from woad was added to turn the cloth green—hence Dyer's Greenweed. An old Yorkshire name was Woadmesh and, before it was replaced by Dyer's Rocket (*Reseda luteola*), and chemical dyestuffs in the 19th century, *Genista* was gathered from the Peak District and sent to Manchester for the dye trade. Some records indicate that the plant was cultivated in the Peak District and it may also have been grown much earlier, by the Romans, in the Glossop area.

Currently, it has a patchy distribution in the Peak, being infrequent in old pastures and by roads and field borders in the Dark Peak but also growing on the tops of limestone ridges (where the calcium content of the soil is not high). The green stems and elongated leaves make it difficult to detect amongst grass, other than between July and September when it produces its showy yellow flowers.

Genista tinctoria is best described as a 'shrublet', with erect, smooth, green stems branching from a brown woody base. It rarely reaches more than 50 cm high. The alternate, stalkless, untoothed leaves are generally hairless except for a marginal fringe. They vary in shape from oval to lanceolate and are up to 3 cm long. The small, bright yellow Broom-like flowers (1–2 cm) are produced near the apex of the branches. The 10 stamens and the central pistil are initially hidden within the fused lower petals until the weight of a foraging bee causes the petals to curl down and release the sexual organs. Bees collect the pollen and aid cross-pollination. The short, flattened pods are usually hairless and (like those of Broom) eject their seeds when they twist open in the sun. Some authorities have divided the group into two subspecies; Peak plants are placed in subspecies *tinctoria*.

A similar plant, which is much rarer in the Peak, is Petty Whin (*Genista anglica*) but this bears spines on the older stems and has broader oval leaves. Both species contain alkaloids and were once used for their diuretic and laxative properties. Dyer's Greenweed is available as a dwarf, double-flowered cultivar and is suitable for rock gardens.

Illustration by Mary Acton

Willow-herb Family *Onagraceae*

Rose-bay Willow-herb *Chamerion angustifolium*

Both the English and Latin names of this plant need explanation! The Willow-herbs (genus *Epilobium*) are a genus of plants with symmetrical flowers and Willow-like leaves with at least the lowest in opposite pairs. This species has slightly asymmetric flowers and spirally produced leaves so it was put in a separate genus, *Chamaenerion*. The name was a combination of 'chamai,' meaning growing on the ground and 'nerion' from a description by the 16th-century botanist, Turner, who thought it looked like Oleander (*Nerium oleander*). The genus name has been changed again, this time to *Chamerion*. Turner's name for Oleander was Rose Bay, hence Rose-bay Willow-herb. It is also known as Fireweed.

Turner thought it was a garden plant but, some 50 years later, Gerard recorded it as growing wild in Yorkshire, from where he introduced it to his garden! In the 1850s the Reverend C.A. Johns stated that it was not often met with in the wild state but was common in gardens. In the last 100 years it has become very common especially in disturbed urban habitats and after fire. It spread along railway lines and flourished in the rubble caused by wartime bombing and later slum clearance. Some authors believe that the sudden explosion in numbers may have been due to a genetic change and not simply an increase in suitable habitats.

Pollen records show that it was common in immediate post-glacial times but that it became rare when much of the country was covered by woodland. Its natural habitats include cliff ledges and scree slopes where it is out of reach of grazing animals. Such habitats are common in the Peak District where it probably survived as a rare wild plant. Today it is locally frequent in woodland clearings and on a range of disturbed habitats.

Erect, tough, unbranched stems (up to 130 cm) are produced from a horizontal, woody rhizome in the spring. These bear long, narrow, smooth, wavy-edged, dark-green leaves which taper at both ends. An unusual feature is that the side veins join with one running just in from the margin (see illustration). The dense, terminal flower heads bear long-stalked flowers with 4 narrow, deep-crimson sepals and 4 rose pink petals. The upper two are often wider than the lower two but this is not always the case. The long thin pods split to release the seeds which are then carried in the wind by a plume of hairs.

As the plant has achieved weed status, the typical form is no longer deliberately grown in gardens but pale-pink and also white cultivars are welcomed in some herbaceous borders.

Illustration by Jacqueline Dawson

Mint Family *Lamiaceae or Labiatae*

Marjoram *Origanum vulgare*

Wild Marjoram was also known as Joy of the Mountains, this being a literal translation of *Origanum* (oros, mountain; and ganos, joy) and for the ancient Greeks it was a symbol of happiness as well as being much used medicinally. In this country it was used as a floor strewing plant and as an ale preservative prior to the introduction of Hop. The dried plant provides us with the culinary herb Oregano but the annual (or biennial) plant grown to provide fresh Marjoram is an African species—*Origanum marjorana*.

Origanum vulgare is a plant of well-drained, infertile soils where there is a high calcium content. It is vulnerable to grazing and trampling so is rarely found on pasture land. It is locally frequent in the limestone dales of the Peak District especially on scree slopes and on sites that have suffered disturbance, for example quarries, burnt grassland, scrub, roadside banks and former cultivated land. It grows with other tall herbs such as Meadow Cranesbill (*Geranium pratense*) and Valerian (*Valeriana officinalis*). It is more frequent on the cooler and moister, north and west facing slopes despite having a deep root system which enables it to reach water in the subsoil layers.

Marjoram is an aromatic perennial with a woody base to its rather stiff, often purple-flushed, downy, erect stem. The plant produces many stems (up to 60 cm high) from its root system, giving it the appearance of a small bush. The pale green, opposite, ovate leaves have occasional teeth at their margins (see illustration). The flowers, which are produced from July to September, are in terminal, flat-topped clusters. Immediately below each flower is a single bract which is larger than the calyx of 5 fused sepals. Both the bract and the sepals are a deep purple colour but the petals are a lighter mauve-pink (occasionally white). Some flowers are bisexual and include 4 protruding stamens. Female flowers also bear stamens but they are tiny, sterile and hidden in the corolla.

The aromatic essential oil extracted from Marjoram contains thymol and is still used both externally (e.g. in aromatherapy and bath oils) and internally (in small amounts) for respiratory disorders, especially coughs, and as a carminative to treat digestive upsets. Marjoram makes a pretty addition to any herb garden, though its oil content is usually well below that of plants from more sunny climates. Popular cultivars include the yellow-leaved 'Aurea' and the curly-leaved 'Crispum'.

Illustration by Geoffrey Copley

Bell Flower family *Campanulaceae*

Harebell *Campanula rotundifolia*

While there is an obvious link between the generic term *Campanula* and the bell-shaped flower of this beautiful plant, the reference to round leaves is more obscure. In fact two sorts of leaves are produced, those on the flowering stems being anything but rounded. Those produced in the shade, at the base of the plant (on non-flowering shoots) are much more rounded, as the illustration clearly shows. There is further confusion over the name Harebell as it was originally used for the plant we now call Bluebell while in parts of the Peak District, *Campanula rotundifolia* was known as Bluebell!

Harebell is found throughout the Peak District on dry, open ground, especially among short turf on the limestone and even on lead mine spoil heaps. It is often associated with Wild Thyme (*Thymus praecox*) and Salad Burnet (*Sanguisorba minor*). Harebell also grows beside roads and on other unproductive habitats (usually on shallow soils) on the gritstone and shale and can put up with a wide range of soil pH. It is late flowering, often not starting until mid July, and carries on well into the autumn.

Harebell is a delicate perennial with both short, non-flowering and longer (to 40 cm) erect, flowering shoots which develop from an underground, creeping stolon. The short shoots produce a cluster of pale-green leaves with long thin petioles and broad, rounded or heart-shaped blades with occasional teeth on the margins. These are mostly hidden by the surrounding vegetation and often die away before the plant finishes flowering. The wiry, slightly sinuous, hairless stem bears alternate, lanceolate leaves, which become smaller, narrower and less toothed towards the stem apex. Each flower is on the end of a very thin stalk and some authors make the link between hair (rather than hare) and bell. As the illustration shows the stalk is erect in the bud stage but then bends over resulting in flowers that nod and tremble in the breeze. The 5, small, dark-green sepals are fused for half their length, the calyx ending in 5 long thin teeth. The 5 petals are fused into a bell shape for up to 75 per cent of their length, the free ends curling back. The thin petals vary in colour from pale to bright blue and often have a slight mauvish tinge. As with Bluebell some plants have white flowers.

Harebell is not common as a garden plant but many other species of *Campanula*, mostly from southern Europe, are grown in herbaceous borders and rock gardens.

Illustration by Lionel Booker

Bell Flower family *Campanulaceae*

Nettle-leaved Bellflower *Campanula trachelium*

There are two large species of wild Bellflower in Britain and both are found in the Peak District. Nettle-leaved Bellflower is named after its Nettle-like leaves but it was also known as Throatwort from the time when its yellow latex was used to treat sore throats and tonsillitis. No doubt the throat-like shape of the flower will have encouraged its early use as a medicinal plant. Another common name is Bats-in-the-belfry on account of the clusters of bell-shaped flowers.

Campanula trachelium is not common in the Peak District where it is found mostly on damp soil in shady sites of the White Peak dales. These are some of its most northerly sites as it has a southern distribution in England. The very similar Giant Bellflower (*Campanula latifolia*) is, in contrast, close to the southern edge of its range where it occurs in similar habitats in the White Peak and also in some Dark Peak woodlands. They are both late flowering species and the flowers rarely emerge before the middle of July.

Nettle-leaved Bellflower produces stout, erect, bristly-haired, little-branched, sharply angled, flowering stems to a height of about 80 cm (those in Giant Bellflower are smoother, bluntly angled and to over a metre). The Nettle-like leaf blades are shaped like the ace of hearts and edged with coarse, irregular pointed teeth. Those below the middle of the stem are borne on petioles. (Giant Bellflower has sessile stem-leaves, shaped like elongated diamonds and with more regularly toothed margins.)

The flowers of *Campanula trachelium* are in clusters of 1–3 in the axils of the leaves, towards the stem apex. Erect in bud, they become more spreading in flower. The hairy, broadly triangular, green calyx teeth contrast with those of *latifolia* which are smooth and narrowly triangular. The bell-like, blue-purple corolla of *trachelium* is up to 3.5 cm long and has 5, broadly triangular, lobes. The larger flowers (up to 5 cm) of *latifolia* are usually paler, with longer, narrower corolla lobes.

Both species are grown in gardens. *Campanula trachelium* 'Bernice' has double flowers and *Campanula latifolia* 'Brantwood' bears deep violet flowers. A similar species, grown in gardens from where it sometimes spreads to the wild, is *Campanula rapunculoides* (Creeping Bellflower). It forms dense clumps and differs in its more slender stem and pendulous flowers.

Illustration by Jennie Hinton

Lily Family *Liliaceae*

Bog Asphodel *Narthecium ossifragum*

The Greek, narthex, meaning a rod, is an apt description of the rigid flower stem of this plant that was originally thought to be a miniature species of Asphodel. Linnaeus put it in the genus *Anthericum* which just happens to be an anagram of its modern genus! The specific name *ossifragum* means 'bone breaker' and comes from the long-held belief (and an earlier name, Cowsick) that animals grazing on the plant would have their bones softened. In fact because the plant grows on pastures devoid of limestone, animals restricted to such land will be prone to brittle bones, due, not to the plant, but to a lack of calcium.

Bog Asphodel is a plant of wet, acid pastures, bogs and moorland flushes (e.g. where a spring emerges) especially in the north and west of Britain but is not common, even where one would expect to find it, in the Dark Peak. Where it does occur it may be locally frequent as in flushes on some of the clough sides (e.g. Jaggers Clough and also near Owler Bar) and it is usually associated with Sphagnum Moss and Cross-leaved Heath (*Erica tetralix*). It is probably under-recorded as it is difficult to spot when not in flower.

Narthecium is a hairless perennial which spreads and forms patches with the break up of its creeping rhizome (see illustration). The plant looks like a miniature Iris as the mostly basal, sword-shaped leaves are held near vertically (often curving as in the illustration). The pale green leaves have parallel veins, are often tipped with orange and (unusually) the lowest leaves are smaller than those higher up. The unbranched, rigid green flower-stem may reach 30 cm but is often only half this height. A few small leaves hug the stem. The flowers, which are produced in late summer and into the autumn, each consist of 6 tepals (3 outer sepals and 3 inner petals that all look alike) bright-yellow on the inner surface but veined with green on the outside. As the illustration shows, these later close up and surround the fruit. The 6 dark orange-red anthers are held on densely pubescent, pale-orange filaments. After flowering, the stem, fruits and remaining floral parts turn a deep saffron-orange and remain in this condition through the winter.

The plant was once used as a cheap substitute for Saffron and was also collected by women to use as a hair dye which gave rise to yet another common name, Maiden's Hair.

Illustration by Mary Acton

Heath family *Ericaceae*

Heather or Ling *Calluna vulgaris*

The Greek word, kallyno, means 'to brush clean' and Calluna has long been used to make besoms. Both Heather and Ling are found as common names in the Peak District; the former originates from a Scottish word, the latter from the old Norse word 'lyng'. Confusingly, Ling is also the name given to a fish (*Molva vulgaris*)! Other old names include Broom (now used for the yellow, pea-flowered shrub) and He-heather.

The development of the Heather moors in the Peak started over 2,500 years ago as a result of a wetter climate and deforestation (possibly maintained by fire and grazing) carried out by Bronze-Age settlers. Today *Calluna* makes up some 20 per cent of the Dark Peak moors, usually on better-drained gritstone sites, where it has long been managed for grouse. These birds require young growth for the best feeding but older growth for nesting and cover for the young. A patchwork of different-aged growth is achieved by controlled spring-time burning of selected areas; this rejuvenates the Heather and kills any tree seedlings, preventing a return to woodland. Heather is killed by the high temperatures of uncontrolled summer fires, overgrazing by sheep and waterlogged soils, where it is replaced by other species. *Calluna* was previously also common on the heaths of the limestone plateau in the White Peak but most of these have now been replaced by grassland.

Heather is a small, evergreen shrub (it can grow up to a metre tall but is commonly much less) with a woody, sinuous stem-base (see illustration) and tiny, sessile, linear leaves produced in opposite pairs (our other Heathers have whorls of leaves and are earlier flowering—see pages 106 and 108). On the short side shoots the leaves overlap, hiding the stem. Most individuals are relatively hairless but some are covered in a dense silvery-grey down. In late summer the terminal flower-spikes change the normally drab moorland into a purple haze of colour. The flowers are in terminal spikes. At the base of each flower are 4 green, or purple, bracts which look like sepals. To add to the confusion the 4 purple-pink sepals look like petals! Inside are the 4, paler, slightly smaller petals that are fused at the base enclosing 8 stamens and a central style.

Heather was much used for fuel, as animal bedding, and even for roof thatching. Bees make a fine Heather honey and the flowers were formerly made into an ale. The lucky white Heather (with pure white flowers and pale green leaves) was popularised by Queen Victoria, who was given a sprig by Albert on their engagement. Many different cultivars are grown in gardens and include a wide range of leaf and flower colours.

Illustration by Primrose Lawton

Glossary

Achene A one-seeded fruit that does not split open.
Adventitious Occurring in a place other than normal.
Alluvial soil That laid down beside streams and rivers from material carried by water.
Annual A plant that completes its life-cycle in 12 months or less.
Appressed Pressed close to (as in hairs to a stem).
Astringent Of a substance that dries and tightens tissue.
Biennial A plant that takes up to 24 months to complete its life-cycle.
Bract A small, modified leaf beneath a flower or flower cluster.
Bulb An underground organ mostly consisting of fleshy leaf-bases.
Bulbil A small bulb or tuber arising from a leaf axil.
Calyx All the sepals.
Carminative A substance that relieves flatulence.
Compound leaf One with a blade of two or more distinct leaflets.
Corm A swollen underground stem, usually erect and arising from the top of that of the previous year.
Corolla All the petals.
Cultivar A cultivated variety.
Deciduous A plant which loses its leaves once a year (usually in autumn in Britain).
Decussate leaves Successive pairs at right-angles to those preceding them.
Dicotyledon Major division of the flowering plants whose members usually have 2 seed leaves (cotyledons). Leaves are usually broad, with net veins and flower parts are in multiples of 4 or 5. (See Monocotyledon.)
Dissected leaf One with the blade deeply cut into different lobes.
Diuretic A substance that promotes the excretion of urine.
Entire leaf One that has margins without lobes or teeth.
Filament The stalk of the pollen-bearing anther.
Follicle A dry fruit that splits open along one side.
Free Not attached to each other (as with petals in some species).
Glabrous Without hairs.
Herb A non-woody plant.
Monocotyledon Major division of the flowering plants whose members usually have only one seed leaf (cotyledon). Leaves are usually narrow, with parallel veins and flower parts are in multiples of 3. (See Dicotyledon.)
Nectary A nectar-secreting gland.
Ovate leaf Oval in shape with a rounded base and pointed apex.
Perennial A plant that lives for more than 2 years. Most perennials flower every year.
Petal Flower part consisting of a modified leaf. Usually brightly coloured and surrounded by sepals.
Petiole Leaf stalk.
Photosynthesis The process by which green plants utilise sunlight to manufacture sugars from water and carbon dioxide.
Pubescent Covered with soft, short hairs.
Reflexed Bent back.
Rhizome An underground stem (often swollen) that lasts for more than one growing season.
Rosette Circular cluster (as of leaves at a stem base).
Sepal Flower part consisting of a modified leaf. Often green and usually external to the petals.
Sessile Not stalked.
Shrub A woody perennial plant that is much branched from near ground level.
Specific epithet Second word of the Latin name of a plant. It is an adjective characterising the species.
Spur A slender (usually hollow) projection from the base of a petal.
Stamen Male part of flower. Made up of pollen-bearing anther and its stalk (filament).
Stigma Apex of the female part of a flower which receives the pollen.
Stipule Leaf-like outgrowth at the base of a petiole. Usually in pairs.
Stolon Creeping stem, usually just above ground.
Style Region of the female part of a flower that connects the stigma with the ovary.
Tannin Astringent substance found in some plants.
Tap root Stout main root that grows vertically.
Tepal Name given to outer flower segments when they are not differentiated into sepals and petals.
Tuber Short-lived, swollen portion of stem or root, not arising from an older one.
Vernal Associated with the spring season.
Vulnerary Substance used for healing wounds.
Wild Type Appearance of the majority of individuals of a species growing in the wild.

Bibliography

Anderson, P., and D. Shimwell, (1981) *Wild Flowers and other Plants of the Peak District*. Moorland.

Baker, M., (1996) *Discovering the Folklore of Plants* (3rd Ed.). Shire Publications.

Brickell, C., (Ed.) (1996) *The Royal Horticultural Society A-Z Encyclopedia of Garden Plants*. Dorling Kindersley.

Clapham, A.R., (1969) *Flora of Derbyshire*. Derby Museum.

Clapham, A.R., T.G. Tutin, and E.F. Warburg, (1962) *Flora of the British Isles* (2nd Ed.). Cambridge University Press.

Culpeper, N., (1653) *The English Physician* or *The Complete Herbal*.

Edwards, K.C., (1962) *The Peak District*. Collins.

Elkington, T. and A. Willmot, (1996) *Endangered Wildlife in Derbyshire*. Derbyshire Wildlife Trust.

Elkington, T. (Ed.) (1986) *The Nature of Derbyshire*. Barracuda Books.

Gerard, J., (1597) *The Herball*. John Norton.

Grieve, M., (1931) *A Modern Herbal*. Jonathan Cape.

Grigson, G., (1955) *The Englishman's Flora*. Phoenix House.

Grigson, G., (1974) *A Dictionary of English Plant Names*. Allen Lane.

Grime, J.P., J.G. Hodgson, and R. Hunt, (1988) *Comparative Plant Ecology: A Functional Approach to Common British Species*. Unwin Hyman.

Harding, P. and G. Tomblin, (1998) *How to Identify Trees*. Harper Collins.

Hulme, F.E., (undated) *Familiar Wild Flowers*. Cassell and Company.

Johns, C.A., (1853) *Flowers of the Field*. S.P.C.K.

Mabey, R., (1996) *Flora Britannica*. Sinclair-Stevenson.

McClintock, D., (1966) *Companion to Flowers*. G. Bell and Sons.

Moss, C.E., (1913) *Vegetation of the Peak District*. Cambridge University Press.

Parkinson, J., (1629) *Paradisi in Sole Paradisus Terrestris*. Humphrey Lownes and Robert Young.

Parkinson, J., (1640) *Theatrum Botanicum*.

Perry, A.R. and R.G. Ellis, (1994) *The Common Ground of Wild and Cultivated Plants*. National Museum of Wales, Cardiff.

Prime, C.T., (1960) *Lords and Ladies*. Collins.

Rose, F., (1981) *The Wild Flower Key*. Frederick Warne.

Shaw, M. (Ed.) (1988) *A Flora of the Sheffield Area*. Sorby Natural History Society.

Index of English Names

(Bold page numbers indicate illustrations)

Alder   20, 58
All-heal   116
Anise   32
Arum, Wild   14, 28, 30, **34**
Ash   50, 56, 60
Ash, Mountain   **56**
Asphodel   134
Avens, Water   **72**
Avens, Wood   72

Bats-in-the-belfry   132
Bear's Foot   18
Bear's Garlic   46
Bellflower, Creeping   132
Bellflower, Giant   132
Bellflower, Nettle-leaved   10, 60, **132**
Bilberry   **42**, 44, 108
Bird's-foot-trefoil   **82**, 84
Bird's-foot-trefoil, Greater   82
Blackberry   110
Blaeberry   42
Blood-drop Emlets   118
Bloody Fingers   120
Bluebell   **30**, 62, 130
Bluebell, Spanish   30
Bog Asphodel   **134**
Bog-heather   106
Box   44, 114
Bracken   30, 32, 42
Bracken, Sweet   32
Broom   54, 124, 136
Broomrape   58
Bulls and Cows   34
Bumble Bee   104
Bunch of Keys   48
Burdock   20
Butterbur   **20**, 32, 118
Buttercup, Bulbous   **40**
Buttercup, Creeping   40
Buttercup, Meadow   40

Cabbage Daisy   64
Campion, Red   76
Campion, Rose   76
Campion, White   78
Carslope   48
Cat-trail   116
Celandine, Greater   22
Celandine, Lesser   6, **22**
Cherry Laurel   36
Cherry, Bird   **36**
Cherry, Wild   36
Christmas Rose   18
Cinquefoil   14, 70
Cinquefoil, Alpine   70
Cinquefoil, Spring   14, **70**

Cloudberry   **110**
Coltsfoot   20
Columbine   **66**
Corpse-flower   58
Cow Parsley   32
Cow Strupple   48
Cowberry   10, 42, **44**, 108
Cowsick   134
Cowslip   **48**
Cranberry   44
Cranesbill, Blood Red   96
Cranesbill, Bloody   78, 94, **96**
Cranesbill, Meadow   64, **94**, 128
Cross-flower   62
Crowfoot, Bulbous   40
Cuckold's Pintle   34
Cuckoo Flower   **26**, 62
Cuckoo Pint   34
Cuckoo Spit   26
Cuckoo's Stockings   30
Culverwort   66

Dead Men's Fingers   90
Deadmen's Bells   120
Dog's Dick   34
Dog's Mercury   34, 98
Dog-tree   50
Dogwood   36
Dovedale Moss   74
Dyer's Greenweed   **124**
Dyer's Rocket   124

Eggs and Bacon   82
Eggs and Collop   82
Elder   50
Elm   58

Fairies Petticoats   120
False Oxslip   48
Figwurt   22
Fireweed   126
Flag, Sweet   122
Flag, Yellow   122
Flowering Box   44
Foxglove   18, 60, **120**
Furze   54

Garlic   46
Garlic, Wild   46
Geranium   78, 94, 96, 128
Globe Flower   10, **64**
Gorse   **54**
Gorse, Western   54
Gowan   64
Grandmother's Toenails   82
Granny's Bonnet   66

Granny's Pincushion   84
Guelder Rose   36, **50**

Hagberry   36
Harebell   30, **130**
Hay Rattle   88
Hazel   50, 58, 60, 64
He-heather   106, 136
Heath, Cross-leaved   **106**, 108, 134
Heath, Irish   106
Heather   6, 13–14, 42, 54, 106, 108, **136**
Heather, Bell   **108**
Heather, Carlin   108
Heckberry   36
Hellebore, Green   **18**
Hellebore, Stinking   18
Hen-penny   88
Herb Paris   60
Hop   128
Horse Chestnut   38
Humble-bee Flower   104

Iris, Yellow   **122**

Jacob's Ladder   14, 64, 74, **98**
Joy of the Mountains   128

Knotberry   110

Lady's Fingers   82, 84
Lady's Slipper   82
Lady's Smock   26, 76
Lamb-toe   84
Laurel   36
Leadwort   15, 68
Lily of the Valley   46, **60**
Ling   15, 54, 106, 108, **136**
Ling, Bell   108
Ling, Crow   108
Long Purples   90
Lucy Locket   26

Maiden's Blush   106
Maiden's Hair   134
Marjoram   78, 94, **128**
May Lily   60
Meadowsweet   98
Milk Maids   26
Mistletoe   54
Mock Orange   102
Moggie-nightgown   24
Money in a Purse   88
Monkey Flower   **118**
Moonwort Fern   68
Musk   118

Myrrh   32
Nipper Nuts   86
Nottingham Catchfly   **78**

Oak   36, 50, 56, 60
Oleander   126
Onion   46, 60
Orchid, Bee   92, 102, **104**
Orchid, Common Spotted   **90**, 102
Orchid, Early-purple   **62**, 90, 102
Orchid, Fly   **92**, 104
Orchid, Fragrant   **102**, 112
Orchid, Frog   15, **114**
Orchid, Heath Spotted   90
Orchid, Marsh   90
Orchid, Pyramidal   102, 104, **112**
Orchid, Spotted   62, 90
Orchis, Early-purple   62
Oxslip   48

Paigle   48
Palsywort   48
Pansy, Garden   68
Pansy, Mountain   15, **68**, 80
Pansy, Wild   68
Peasling   86
Penny-grass   88
Perennial Sweet Pea   86
Petty Whin   124
Pilewort   22
Plantain, Greater   100
Plantain, Hoary   **100**
Polyanthus   48
Poppy   120
Primrose   48, 84, 108, 136

Quicken   56

Ragged Robin   26, **76**
Ramshorns   46
Ramsons   20, 28, **46**, 60
Raspberry   110
Rock-rose, Common   14, **80**
Rose   18, 36, 52, 56, 70, 72, 110
Rose Elder   50
Rowan   **56**

Saffron   134
Salad Burnet   84, 130
Saxifrage, Fingered   74
Saxifrage, Meadow   **74**
Saxifrage, Mossy   74
Saxifrage, White   74
Scent Bottle   100
She-heather   106
Silverweed   70
Smell Fox   24
Snowball Tree   50
Sphagnum Moss   106, 134
Spring Messenger   22
Staunch   84
Strawberry, Alpine   52
Strawberry, Barren   52
Strawberry, Garden   52
Strawberry, Wild   **52**
Sunflower   80
Sweet Cicely   20, **32**
Sweet William   76

Thistle, Stemless   10
Throatwort   132
Thunderclouds   94
Toadflax   38
Toothwort   **58**

Umbrella Leaves   20

Valerian   64, 98, **116**, 128
Valerian, Greek   98
Valerian, Red   116
Vernal Sandwort   15, 68
Vetch, Bitter   **86**
Vetch, Horseshoe   84
Vetch, Kidney   **84**
Violet, Common Dog   **38**
Violet, Early Dog   38
Violet, Heath   38
Violet, Sweet   38

Wake Robin   34
Water Elder   50
Water Forget-me-not   118
Water-Crowfoot   40
Weasel Snout   28
Whin   54, 124
White Deadnettle   28
Whitebeam   56
Whortleberry   42, 44
Whortleberry, Red   44
Wild Hyacinth   30
Wild Rhubarb   20
Wild Service Tree   56
Wild Thyme   130
Wild William   76
Willow   20
Willow-herb, Rose-bay   **126**
Willow-herbs   126
Windflower   24
Wintergreen   15
Woad   124
Woadmesh   124
Wood Anemone   **24**, 28, 46
Wood Sorrel   24

Yellow Archangel   **28**, 34, 46
Yellow Rattle   14, **88**

Index of Latin Names

Acorus calamus   122
Allium ursinum   20, 28, **46**
Alnus glutinosa   20, 58
Anacamptis pyramidalis   **112**
Anemone nemorosa   **24**, 28, 46
Anthericum   134
Anthriscus sylvestris   32
Anthyllis vulneraria   **84**
Aquilegia vulgaris   **66**
Arctium spp.   20
Arum maculatum   14, 28, **34**

Botrychium lunaria   68
Buxus sempervirens   44

Calluna vulgaris   13, 15, 54, **136**
Campanula latifolia   132
Campanula rapunculoides   132
Campanula rotundifolia   **130**
Campanula trachelium   10, 60, **132**
Cardamine pratensis   **26**, 62, 76
Centranthus ruber   116
Chamaenerion   126
Chamerion angustifolium   **126**
Chelidonium majus   22
Cirsium acaulon   10
Cistus   80
Coeloglossum viride   15, **114**
Convallaria majalis   **60**
Cornus sanguinea   36
Corylus avellana   50, 58

Dactylorhiza fuchsii   **90**
Dactylorhiza maculata   90
Digitalis purpurea   **120**

Endymion   30
Epilobium   126
Erica cinerea   **108**
Erica mackaiana   106
Erica tetralix   **106**, 108, 134

Filipendula vulgaris   98
Fragaria vesca   **52**
Fragaria × ananassa   52
Fraxinus excelsior   50, 56
Fuchsia   90

Galeobdolon luteum   28
Genista anglica   124
Genista tinctoria   **124**
Geranium pratense   **94**, 128
Geranium sanguineum   78, **96**
Geum chiloense   72
Geum coccineum   72
Geum rivale   **72**
Geum urbanum   72

Geum × intermedium   72
Gymnadenia conopsea   **102**

Helianthemum chamaecistus   80
Helianthemum nummularium   14, **80**, 84
Helianthus annuus   80
Helleborus foetidus   18
Helleborus niger   18
Helleborus viridis   **18**
Hippocrepis comosa   84
Hyacinthoides hispanica   30
Hyacinthoides non-scripta   **30**
Hyacinthus   30, 60
Hydrangea   50

Iris pseudacorus   **122**

Lamiastrum galeobdolon   **28**, 34, 46
Lamium galeobdolon   28
Lathraea squamaria   **58**
Lathyrus latifolius   86
Lathyrus linifolius   **86**
Lathyrus montanus   86
Lotus corniculatus   **82**, 84
Lotus pedunculatus   82
Lychnis coronaria   76
Lychnis flos-cuculi   **76**

Mercurialis perennis   34, 98
Mimulus guttatus   **118**
Mimulus luteus   118
Mimulus moschatus   118
Minuartia verna   15, 68
Myosotis scorpiodes   118
Myrrhis odorata   20, **32**

Narthecium ossifragum   **134**
Nerium oleander   126

Ophrys apifera   **104**
Ophrys insectifera   **92**
Ophrys muscifera   92
Orchis mascula   **62**
Origanum marjorana   128
Origanum vulgare   78, **128**
Oxalis acetosella   24

Paris quadrifolia   60
Pelargonium   94
Petasites hybridus   **20**, 32, 118
Philadelphus   102
Plantago major   100
Plantago media   **100**
Plantago nivalis   100
Polemonium caeruleum   14, **98**
Potentilla anserina   70

Potentilla crantzii   70
Potentilla neumanniana   14, **70**
Potentilla sterilis   52
Potentilla tabernaemontani   70
Potentilla verna   70
Primula elatior   48
Primula veris   **48**
Prunus avium   36
Prunus laurocerasus   36
Prunus padus   **36**
Pyrola minor   15

Quercus petraea   50

Ranunculus acris   40
Ranunculus bulbosus   **40**
Ranunculus ficaria   **22**
Ranunculus repens   40
Reseda luteola   124
Rhinanthus crista-galli   88
Rhinanthus minor   14, **88**
Rubus chamaemorus   **110**
Rubus idaeus   110

Salix spp.   20
Sambucus nigra   50
Sanguisorba minor   84, 130
Saxifraga granulata   **74**
Saxifraga hypnoides   74
Saxifraga tridactylites   74
Scilla   30
Silene dioica   76
Silene latifolia   78
Silene nutans   **78**
Sorbus aucuparia   **56**

Thlaspi alpestre   15
Thymus praecox   130
Trollius europaeus   10, **64**
Tussilago farfara   20

Ulex europaeus   **54**
Ulex gallii   54
Ulmus glabra   58
Vaccinium myrtillus   13, **42**, 108
Vaccinium oxycoccus   44
Vaccinium vitis-idaea   10, 42, **44**, 108
Vaccinium × intermedium   42
Valeriana officinalis   98, **116**, 128
Viburnum opulus   36, **50**
Viola canina   38
Viola lutea   15, **68**
Viola odorata   38
Viola reichenbachiana   38
Viola riviniana   **38**
Viola tricolor   68

General Index

Ancient Woodland   24, 86
Aphrodisiac   62
Aphrodite   24
Apollo   30

Bach Flower Remedies   80, 118
Besom   54
Bradford Dale   18
Bronze-age   136
Bumble Bee   104
Buxton   9, 12, 15–16

Cancer   30
Carboniferous era   11
Carminative   32, 128
Chartreuse   32
Cheedale   70
Chesterfield   7, 16, 116
Clough   108, 134
Common Frog   114
Cromford Canal   118, 122
Culpeper, Nicholas   66, 98

Deep Dale   66
Derby   9, 16
Derbyshire   9, 11, 24, 26, 54, 92, 112, 116
Derwent Valley   110
Diarrhoea   18, 42, 52
Dioscorides   32
Diuretic   32, 124
Doctrine of signatures   74
Douglas, David   118
Dovedale   74, 78

Easter   54
Eczema   40
Eyam   42

Fowlers   56
Fuchs, Leonard   90, 120

Genesis   98
Gerard, John   36, 38, 50, 64, 74, 76, 80, 86, 104, 110, 126
Glossop   12, 16, 124

Green Hairstreak   82
Grouse   14, 42, 110, 136

Hartington   12, 114
High Peak   9–10, 14
Honey   104, 136
Hopton   104
House-fly   92
Huddersfield   9, 16

Iron Age   14

Jaggers Clough   134
Johns, C.A.   126
Jonson, Ben   52

Kinder Scout   10

Lathkill Dale   9, 98
Laxative   52, 100, 124
Lead spoil   40, 112
Lead workings   90
Leek   9, 12, 16
Linnaeus, Carl   106, 118, 134
Longstone Edge   102
Louis VII   122
Low Peak   9

Manchester   9, 16, 124
Manifold Valley   60
May Day   60
Miller's Dale   78, 96, 102, 104
Milton, John   48
Monsal Head   60

Nottingham castle   78

Ophelia   66, 68
Orange Tip butterfly   26
Owler Bar   134

Padley Gorge   14, 42
Parkinson, John   66
Pied Piper   116
Plague   40
Pliny   22, 104
Pleiocene era   11

Portland sago   34

Quarries   15, 40, 52, 90, 102, 104, 112, 114, 116, 128
Queen Victoria   136

Railways   15, 114
Ravensdale   60
Ray, John   78
Rendzina   13
River Derwent   20, 32, 110, 118
River Dove   20, 118
River Wye   20, 32, 64, 118
Robin Goodfellow   34, 76

Sedative   18, 36
Six-spot Burnet Moth   82, 112
Shakespeare, William   26, 66, 68, 90, 100
Sheffield   5–7, 9, 12, 16, 42
Silage   13–14, 74, 88
Site of Special Scientific Interest   15, 92, 112
Small Blue butterfly   84
Solitary Wasp   92
Sough   11
Southwell Minster   70
Staffordshire   9, 42, 46
Starch   30, 34

Thatching   136
Tideswell Dale   86
Turner, William   22

Valerie growers   116
Valium   116
Via Gellia   14, 102
Vitamin c   52

Well dressing   40
Whooping cough   36
Willisel, Thomas   78
Withering, William   120
Wordsworth, William   22, 68
Wormhill   18
Wye Valley   64